GOD KNOWS
YOUR NAME

GOD KNOWS YOUR NAME

GREG BUDD

WINEPRESS WP PUBLISHING

WinePress Publishing (PO Box 428, Enumclaw, WA 98022) functions only as book publisher. As such, the ultimate design, content, editorial accuracy, and views expressed or implied in this work are those of the author.

ISBN 1-57921-836-9

Library of Congress Catalog Card Number: 2005911144

DEDICATION

—➤«(●)»◄—

I would like to dedicate this book to my wife, Lesa. It has been my privilege to watch God in action through her ministry. Her passion for reaching hurting people with the gospel has been a constant inspiration to me. Lesa, thank you for twenty-five wonderful years of marriage and shared ministry. God has used you to encourage others in many creative ways. You have enriched the faith of many who have felt like giving up. People lost in darkness and despair now know "God Knows Your Name." I am sure you will enjoy eternity with the many smiling faces you have helped along the way. May God continue to anoint you with His grace as you lift up His Son before a lost and dying world.

TABLE OF CONTENTS

PREFACE

—⟫•⟨—

God Knows Your Name was written as an encouragement for those struggling with the challenges of life. At times they can feel insurmountable. An increasing number of people feel insignificant and forgotten as they try to just make it through the overwhelming difficulty that faces them.

Our world is more connected today than ever before. At the same time a sense of disconnectedness abounds. People working across the aisle from each other in high-tech office buildings communicate a good morning by e-mail rather than exchanging simple greetings. We walk up and down busy streets in our own world, insulated by headphones. Families rarely sit down to enjoy a meal together. Instead they sit collectively staring at the television without any meaningful dialogue. We race in and out of airports, to work, to school, and a host of other activities demanding our attention. In our frantic pace we seldom have time to talk. We travel the highway, engaged in cell phone conversation; we fly by the wildflowers in bloom, not even realizing they are there. If the birds still sing in the park we can't be sure. Rare are ice cream socials with three-legged races. Families no longer need to gather around the wood stove; we have climate control systems providing perfect temperature year round. In many ways relationships have been replaced by technology.

As my wife and I attempt to encourage and strengthen faith, we encounter the product of our disconnected society. People are overwhelmed. Discouragement and depression have become familiar companions for many. Feeling forgotten and alone, they conclude that God must have forgotten them as well. It is my desire that the following true life experiences will strengthen and encourage all who read them. The individuals in these stories come from a variety of circumstances and places. Each story is a powerful testimony that God has not forgotten their name.

As an introduction to these stories, listen to the voice of God through His written word: "So that you may know that it is I, the Lord, the God of Israel, who calls you by your name. For the sake of Jacob, My servant, and Israel, My chosen one, I have also called you by your name; I have given you a title of honor" (Isa. 45:3–4).

Do you know you were chosen by God? Do you know that God has a special place in His heart reserved just for you? He desires for you to accept your title in the royal family. It is my prayer as you read the experiences of ordinary men and women in this book you will hear God say, "So that you may know that it is I, the God of Israel, who calls you by your name."

In a world specializing in feelings of insignificance, it is good news to know that you are significant to the God of heaven! In a world filled with pain and suffering of every kind, it is so encouraging to know you are not alone in your suffering; your Lord suffers with you. In a world with increasing disaster and destruction, you can find hope in a God who would come on such an amazing rescue mission for someone like you and me.

If your life has been characterized by heartache and pain in the places you should have experienced love and acceptance; if you feel God has somehow misplaced your name and you are forgotten and alone, He speaks these words to you:

"Can a woman forget her nursing child and have no compassion on the son of her womb? Even these may forget, but I will not forget you. Behold, I have inscribed you on the palms of My hands" (Isa. 49:15–16).

Your name has been etched for eternity onto the hands of God! He will never leave you nor forsake you! As you contemplate His gift of love to you, gratitude and thanksgiving will replace your despair. Wouldn't you like to join your voice with mine, thanking Him for His amazing grace and the eternal inscription of your name in the palm of His hands? You can be forever certain, "God Knows Your Name."

ACKNOWLEDGMENTS

I would like to thank each individual featured in this book. I am confident your story will be a blessing to many.

Jeannie Buchholz also deserves a special thank you for editorial assistance. The many long hours invested in this project are much appreciated.

All real tribute is directed to our loving Heavenly Father. Your personal interest and providential leading in the lives of the persons featured in the following pages provide us with new courage and faith. May these examples serve as a fresh reminder of who You really are.

JOE

———⸎⸎———

In September of 1998 we watched with a feeling of helplessness as Hurricane George slammed into island after island, shredding everything in its path. Antigua was first to feel the power and devastation from this giant mass of twisting, churning air. George's 150 mph winds made splinters of the modest homes in Antigua. As buildings disintegrated, the black angry clouds opened their floodgates, dumping inches of rain on helpless victims and causing little streams and city streets to become raging torrents. The survivors were stunned and dazed as they bid farewell to George.

George continued his deadly course of destruction. The U.S. Virgin Islands promised to be another direct hit. The stunned victims stared in disbelief as George left their islands in shambles, roaring on in the direction of Puerto Rico. Without mercy the relentless storm repeated its fury in Puerto Rico, Dominican Republic, Haiti, and Cuba. Most of George's fury abated by the time it made land in Key West, Florida.

It is impossible to comprehend the heartache and sorrow of the survivors left in the wake of incredible disaster. Six hundred two people had lost their lives in this storm, with the majority from the Dominican Republic and Haiti. Destruction was inevitable as the eye of the hurricane passed directly over the center of their island. Pictures of sobbing people digging through feet of mud with entombed loved ones haunted our family. The people we were watching on the news could have been our neighbors. For almost two years we lived and worked with the people of the Dominican Republic at a small mission school situated directly in the path of this monster storm. With communication to the hardest-hit areas completely cut off, all we could do was wait. We wondered what had happened to our friends at the little mission school.

The voice on the other end of the telephone resounded with urgency. "The mission school has taken a direct hit. The eye of angry Hurricane George passed directly over us. Every roof has been stripped from the buildings. We look through gaping openings to the sky. The beautiful tropical trees lie twisted and shredded. Now they look more like a giant game of pick up sticks than the beautiful campus you left a short time ago. The rains have continued to pour on the nearly drowned students and faculty. Most of what was not blown away is exposed to flooding rain. People are huddled under plastic tarps in the jungle, waiting for someone to come and help. How soon can you come?"

I agreed to be part of a disaster relief team that would come as soon as possible.

Picturing families with small children, teachers, and students huddling under plastic tarps definitely hastened preparations for travel. The next morning as I went into the bathroom to brush my teeth, I was startled by a voice with some very explicit instructions. "Take Joe Crary with you to the Dominican Republic."

Surprised and somewhat startled, I wondered, "What was that all about? Did I just hear God telling me to take Joe Crary with me to the Dominican Republic?"

Then it came again, "Take Joe Crary with you to the Dominican Republic."

"OK Lord," I said. "I will talk to his dad about it today." I wondered what was happening in Joe's life that would cause God to initiate such a plan. After explaining my strange encounter to Mark and Janelle Crary, Joe's parents, they agreed that it would be an excellent experience. God must be working on a special plan for Joe's life.

Joe was a wiry and muscular young teen with energy to burn. He was a good kid with an unusually generous heart. He literally would give away the shirt from his back. As a small boy he would gladly share what he had if someone wanted it, even something as precious as ice cream. From time to time the family would stop for a treat at the Dairy Queen. If someone would ask in fun for a bite of his ice cream cone, Joe would smile and hand them his cone.

Joe was just beginning the wonderful time in life that parents look forward to, adolescent independence. It is at this moment teens declare that one more day must not pass without defining their identity. If tomorrow should arrive and they had not done their part raising the flag of independence, surely the whole of the teen kingdom would see them as weak. The cause of freedom has no room for non-contributors.

Joe was feeling all the typical desires for independence and self-government teens bless their parents with during the breaking away period. One of the struggles that needed clarification in Joe's mind was church attendance. "I am thirteen now. I should be old enough to decide for myself if I want to go to church!" These contests, determining who was charge, usually ended peaceably with Mom and Dad still holding the reins for their thirteen-year-old going on thirty. Joe felt like many young people growing up in Christian homes—he just wanted to find out who God was for himself. Joey really was a good kid. He just happened to be born on planet earth with all the growing pains of childhood to manhood.

It was in the midst of this restlessness that God instructed me to invite Joe to accompany me on the SOS mission to the Dominican Republic. At the very time that Joe thought he might need a little vacation from God, God planned a little vacation for him. Joe was ready to go the minute Mom and Dad explained the need for his assistance. The thought of helping people, combined with a visit to a tropical island, seemed like a winning plan. Once travel arrangements and documents were in hand, he was chomping at the bit to get going. Mom and Dad helped pack his bags, and he was ready.

With a hug and kiss goodbye from Mom and Dad, Joe was ready to board the plane. He determined such behavior must be appropriate, as he had seen other men, even older than himself, participate in such farewell activities. Even though this day had a very early beginning, Joe was anything but tired. He was on his first flight out of the country. Joe stared out the window at the fleecy wonderland beneath him. From time to time the clouds would part, displaying the landscape below. The adventure just ahead made it seem like only a few minutes until we heard the stewardess invite us to prepare for landing in Miami.

As we boarded our next plane, instructions in Spanish reminded us we were on our way to another country. In a moment we were airborne and the scenery below us changed immediately. The beautiful Caribbean Sea sparkled and danced. The little islands accenting beautiful turquoise waters held a romance all its own. Ships of all sizes carving their way through white capped waves added to the picturesque image. The young adventurer seated beside me kept his eyes close to the window. After passing over numerous little islands and the corner of Cuba, we began our descent. The mountains of Haiti greeted us for a few moments before descending into the Dominican Republic. The runways of Santo Domingo came into view as we made our final descent. Looking out the window as we taxied down the runway provided us with a new perspective. The recent hurricane had changed this little island into a war zone!

Fred Flint, the mission president, and a student welcomed us as we cleared customs. Warm tropical air greeted us as we walked through the airport to the parking lot. From the airport on the coastline we began our journey to the central portion of the island. What a sight greeted our eyes! The beautiful palm trees gracefully adorning the coastline and nearby highway were now in a twisted, tangled mess. Many trees had been uprooted and hurled across the highway. As we began our slow and tedious trek, we often had to come a complete stop to negotiate the narrow openings sawn through fallen trees. Signs of flooding were everywhere. Small houses with standing water around them dotted the landscape. Little ravines that had been seasonal streams turned into raging rivers. Everything in their path had been carried away. Joe stared out the window, trying to process the enormity of the devastation. Tornadoes from time to time in the Midwest cut small paths through a town or countryside, but this was like a tornado without boundaries. An entire island had been ravaged. The further we traveled, the worse the devastation.

Finally we reached the last village at the end of the highway-road-path we had been traveling on. This little village had been a bull's-eye for Hurricane George. Even in the darkness we could see massive destruction all around us. This poor little town had nearly been erased from the map. Leaving town, the road steadily deteriorated. As we passed the outskirts of the town and over a concrete bridge spanning a small river, Fred tried to point out in the dim light the enormity of the floodwaters just a few days earlier. This little river of a few feet deep had grown into a raging torrent with several feet of water flowing over the bridge. We crept on, winding our way around fallen trees and washed-out areas of the road. This last thirteen kilometers was nearly impassable during certain times of the year, and a hurricane certainly had not improved matters.

It was late as we pulled onto the mission grounds. At the end of a very long day, we were ready for a good night's sleep. Now it was our turn to pray for good weather. We were shown to our bunks in one of the buildings with a makeshift roof. Looking at the stars shining through the openings above us was not all that assuring. If it rained, every fourth raindrop would probably be diverted to our beds. In a few moments we fell fast asleep with scarcely a thought that any living creature from the jungle surrounding us could enter at will. Even moving, slithering objects could not keep us awake—we were tired!

The clang of the morning gong awoke us to the new day and the opportunity to inspect some of the damage first hand. Leaving Joe alone to squeeze the last hour from the sheets, I joined the small group of worshipers for a morning praise and devotional. One would have never known that much of what this band of cheery worshipers possessed had vanished. Their faces simply radiated with an inner joy and happiness. When the worship ended, I was sure I had been the one to receive the encouragement, rather than the one bringing it.

Breakfast would be served in just a few minutes. I was sure that Joe, being a full-fledged adolescent, would not want to break the sleeping code by getting out of bed on his own. He may need a little help. I approached the lifeless form buried under the blanket rather apprehensively until I remembered that I had a very advantageous weapon called food. Joe was in full compliance to the adolescent code—sleeping in as late as possible. His comrades back at home would have been proud of him, had they been able to observe him. The airplane meals the day before had not exactly reminded Joe of Thanksgiving. With one eye open, his youthful appetite propelled him from his little nest toward the cafeteria.

It was not hard to read Joe's dreaming eyes; he was ready for a big breakfast! Reaching the cafeteria, we took our place in line with Joe still rubbing his eyes and trying to decide if he had been extricated from his haven of rest prematurely. The cafeteria line moved slowly to the serving area. Joe just stared in disbelief. "What is that?" he asked warily.

On display for the choosing were several varieties of steaming tubers of all sizes, shapes, and colors. "These are roots from the garden that are grown kind of like potatoes," I replied.

"Purple potatoes," was all Joe said, as he continued to stare at what he hoped was only a bad dream. He didn't say it, but I could read his thoughts, "Where are the pop tarts? Where are the Frostie O's? Has anyone ever heard of cinnamon rolls or bagels? Where are the hash browns and pancakes? There isn't even any orange juice or milk." In one slow but deliberate about-face, Joe backtracked to the beginning of the line, restacked his tray on the pile, and walked out the door.

Money was scarce at the little mission, with basic items making up the menu even in better times; now the garden was gone. Fruits and vegetables alike had been destroyed. It would be a time of survival until nature could recover.

Blain Robison had also responded to the SOS. Blain, with his wife and family, had previously lived at the mission, helping to finish some of the projects under construction. Carl and Debbie Norris had come to the little mission on a two-week project the year before. They also wanted to be a part of the encouraging and rebuilding. Together, as an evaluation team, we walked from building to building looking at the damaged roofs. The rafters were twisted in heaps or missing altogether. The roofing that could be located looked like tin foil wrapped around branches in the trees. Where to begin? We attempted to prioritize projects to determine which should receive the most immediate attention. With a few basic goals established, the work began.

Before we knew it the gong sounded for lunch. Joe was hopeful as he entered the cafeteria for another try for some real food. I couldn't help noticing Joe's face as he surveyed the lunch menu. The menu had been varied from breakfast by rotating the shapes and colors of the root varieties into different formations than had been served at breakfast. Poor Joe, he simply could not believe his eyes as he looked at the newly organized tubers. He shook his head, repeated the morning process of returning his tray to its resting place and walked out the door. Tempted to feel a bit disappointed, I reminded myself I would be returning home in few days, but this would be reality for everyone here for some time to come.

Feeling responsible and a bit concerned for Joe's empty stomach, I decided I had better find him and see how he was doing without any food. Joe was sitting by his suitcase munching contentedly when I found him. "Joe, what are you eating?" I asked.

"My dad made me some trail mix in case I might get hungry," he replied. His suitcase was full of food; it looked like someone had robbed a nut factory. A wide variety of other food treasures accompanied his suitcase full of trail mix. After two meals of roots, Joe's lunch looked pretty good. "Where did Joe's dad get a recipe for ten gallons of trail mix?" I wondered. All sympathy for Joe vanished upon the discovery of his stash. Now it was my turn to turn and walk away, with an almost empty stomach, from Joe's dining hall.

The afternoon was spent with further straightening of rafters and applying plastic tarps as temporary roofing. As we finished for the day, Joe decided this would be the time to put up his one-man pup tent. This would be his private fortress against adults attempting to penetrate his adolescent kingdom. Joe also concluded that he might need fortification against spiritual influences that could attempt access to his kingdom. After moving his portable grocery store-suitcase and bedding to his tent-fortress, he looked like a man who had just staked out a claim on the frontier. The only thing missing was a mascot and a flag flying over his doorway.

With a little rearranging in the daylight, all of us felt more prepared for the hours of darkness. The sun goes down early near the equator. It was about six thirty when the sun left the sky, leaving few options to those who enjoy the luxury of light. With the nearest electricity several kilometers away, many distractions are non-existent. We were anxious to hear first hand from those who had weathered the ferocious storm. This seemed like an excellent time to share stories of God's providence.

One by one the students and faculty joined us for an evening of stories filled with praise to God for His wonderful protection. We arranged our chairs in a small circle with a flickering candle as our centerpiece. "Tell us, what was a hurricane with 150 mph winds coming directly at you like?" I asked.

One of the ladies attempted to describe her experience. "All the women gathered in the bathroom of the blockhouse behind us," she said motioning to the house only a few feet from our circle. "The sky turned dark and the winds began to blow harder and harder. All at once we heard what sounded like the roaring of a freight train with enormous winds pounding and shrieking at us. We were terrified by sounds not only outside but by the sounds of the creaking, groaning house. We waited anxiously, hoping that our defense would not suddenly disappear, leaving us to the fury of the storm. We began to pray, asking God to send angels excelling in strength to surround and protect us. We felt an almost immediate answer to our prayers. As an amazing sensation of peace swept over us, we began to sing. Louder and louder we sang, praising God in the midst of the storm.

"After an hour or so, everything became deathly still as the eye of Hurricane George hovered directly over us. We waited anxiously for what we knew would come. Without warning, the winds that had been blowing from one direction exploded upon us from the opposite direction. The roof gave one momentary shudder and with a crackling sound disappeared into the sky. Then torrential rains poured in on us; it felt like we were being attacked by a powerful force. We knew the devil would love to destroy this little mission. It had been a source of help for many people with physical, medical, and spiritual needs. God's gift of peace surrounded us, so we sang on in the pouring rain."

I looked over at the little pup tent-fortress pitched just a few feet away. Joe had retreated to his tent, attempting to remain somewhat independent from this time of praise and thanksgiving to God. After all, part of the reason he had come on this trip was to take a little break from God. Joe let us know how he was feeling by absenting himself from all spiritual activity. At first I wasn't sure if I should invite Joe to join in at worship or not. As I pondered how best to reach Joe, I had a very strong impression: "Don't say a word to Joe. I am able to reach him without your help. Just leave him to Me." I was sure God knew what He was doing, so I just waited and watched to see what would happen. I could see the little tent move from time to time, knowing Joe could not fall asleep at 7:30 p.m. even if he tried. It was plain to see that Joe could not help hearing the stories detailing the providence of God. I knew Joe must be going stir crazy, zipped in his little tent, now turned into a prison. He was trying to hide from God with his tent pitched just a few feet from what could have been a church pulpit, blessed by one speaker after another.

As one of the men began to describe the storm, I noticed out of the corner of my eye the zipper on the little pup tent begin to slowly move downward. In a moment or two Joe's face appeared, looking intently in the direction of the person speaking. The men had taken refuge in a small concrete tool room built like a vault inside the large chapel. How they fit all those bodies inside an enclosure eight feet by eight feet seemed like an impossibility. We could only imagine what it must have been like being entombed with several men pressed tightly together in a room with no air movement at ninety-five degrees for several hours. Fresh air had never been appreciated by this group of men as much as it was the moment the door opened.

A smile broke across the face of the tent dweller as he played back the reality of the tool room experience. After a few more versions of the storm, it was off to bed. The morning sun would greet us all too soon. Crowing roosters—engaging in predawn vocal exercises at least two hours before the sun shed its first beams of light—would be our alarm clock.

The next morning Joe not only opted from the worship hour, he didn't even bother carrying an empty tray to the food display and returning it to the stack. I really didn't feel too sorry for Joe at mealtime after discovering his mini-mart grocery store suitcase. I tried to decide if, not coveting anything that was my neighbor's, included the articles in Joe's suitcase. It was a tough call with roots and more roots.

Roofing materials had been sold out on the entire island almost immediately after the storm. The entire country was waiting for the next shipment to arrive. The best we could do for the time being was replace or repair rafters and fasten temporary tarps. It was very hot and humid working in the tropical sun. We looked forward to the cool of sunset and the opportunity to hear more stories of God's providence.

By the light of the moon and a small lantern, our small story hour praise session assembled. Blain Robison began to share his conversion story. Blain had been causally interacting with Joe much like a big brother as we worked throughout the day. This time Joe decided to chance listening outside the protection of his fortress and actually joined the small circle for the moonlight story hour. I could sense God was using Blain to speak to Joe as he tailored the stories of his youth and his attempt to run from God.

Blain openly shared the pain and disillusionment that accompanied his search for pleasure and happiness apart from God. The further he went from God, the more miserable he felt. Blain had totally miscalculated a woman who knew her way well to the throne of grace. The power of his mother's prayers followed him wherever he went. After many years of running, he realized he would never escape a God who would not let him go.

I watched Joe out of the corner of my eye from across the little circle in the moonlight as Blain described the joy and happiness that discovering Jesus had brought to his life. It was quiet for a few minutes after Blain finished and Joe seemed thoughtful as he reflected on the decisions he was facing in his life. He had traveled thousands of miles to escape his parents' prayers and here he sat listening to a testimony that was like an arrow aimed at his heart. Joe was beginning to discover the same lesson Blain had discovered: praying parents are impossible to escape. No matter how far you run or where you might try to hide, God is always there, inviting you to come back to Him!

Each day the sun seemed to be strengthening its intensity. The heat became more and more difficult to endure. The sweltering temperatures left us feeling exhausted at the end of the day. The cool of the evening came as a welcome relief. Each evening the stories shared were like arrows aimed at Joe's heart. All the while he had to know that these people could never have known God was using them to speak to a young man trying to define his identity. This evening would be no exception.

Daniel and Nick, two students attending the training program at the mission, had miraculously escaped the horrors of Haiti. Their stories came from a totally different perspective. The whole idea of God being in charge of your life was at the center of Joe's struggles. It seemed like those living life without Him had a lot more freedom and happiness. Daniel and Nick told story after story of growing up in a country that had rejected God and had endorsed voodoo, a religion of darkness, as their god. Horrors beyond description were everyday realities for those unfortunate persons born in a country rejecting God and worshiping darkness. Riots and bloodshed were common responses from a whole nation without hope. Evil spirits masquerading as dead persons walking the streets were common occurrences. Without God's blessing, the majority could expect to die of starvation or sickness. Daniel and Nick beamed as they recounted God's miraculous intervention on their behalf. They had managed to cross the border from Haiti into the Dominican Republic, which is almost impossible for Haitians. They repeated over and over what a difference knowing Jesus had made. Their lives, once filled with sadness, despair, starvation, and hopelessness, were now filled with joy and happiness.

Once again Joe looked thoughtful for a long time after they finished recounting their experiences. As people asked the two Haitian students for further details, Joe seemed lost in thought. This picture of a whole country living their lives apart from God seemed anything but inviting. Was it possible that God was not the freedom-stealing God he had supposed? A hundred required church services by Mom and Dad could never have spoken so directly to Joe's heart as the personal testimonies he heard from night to night.

The next night provided further enlightenment for the questions Joe was struggling with. Fun, adventure, and excitement— Christians seemed to be missing them all in Joe's estimation. God used Blain once again to dispel the misconceptions that Joe was beginning to believe about God and the quality of life He provides. Joe was like so many young people who see the lights and hear the music of the world, thinking life will surely pass them by if they follow God. The devil is constantly telling all who will listen that God's way of life will be dull and boring. If you follow God, your life will lack the adventure and fun that He alone can provide.

Blain began his story of the evening with the preface, "What an adventure I have had since I decided to follow Jesus. I thought I would find adventure in the world, but it was nothing compared with the adventures God has led me on.

"A short time after our adventure in the Dominican Republic, I received a phone call inviting me to New Guinea as part of a team that would be filming a documentary. We would need to travel many miles into the interior by canoe to film the history of one of the first missionaries to New Guinea. God has allowed me to travel and work for Him around the world. Talk about adventure; let me tell you about adventure. After gathering our equipment from the plane we were transported to the edge of an enormous river that is the super highway to the interior. A fifty-foot dugout canoe waited to take us to our destination. We loaded all our film equipment into this hollowed out log and we were off. What a sensation, trying to balance a whole crew, film equipment, barrels of fuel, food, and water on a fifty-foot hollow tree that felt like it could roll upside down at any moment. The current was strong as we journeyed deep into the interior.

"After several hours we encountered a strong crosscurrent that began to move our floating log around in the river at will. We looked carefully at each floating log, as the river was full of crocodiles. Without warning, the current took our canoe and spun it around like a cork and then flipped us upside down. I found myself bobbing near the capsized canoe, being swept along by the strong current."

I looked over at Joe. He was sitting on the edge of his seat. He could feel the action and adventure. There seemed to be very little that could resemble boring and dull at this moment. Blain was helplessly bobbing along with the precious cargo that was buoyant enough to stay afloat.

"Every sensation of underwater objects brushing against my legs caused me to wonder if I would be drug under by a giant crocodile."

Joe looked like he was the one floating down the river, with a very wide awake look on his face reflecting in the shadows of the moonlight. He listened intently to the rescue as the natives along the banks began to send signals up the river on their drums much the way they did when the first missionaries made their way into the interior. Joe sat captivated, listening to the way God rescued His floating missionaries without a single person becoming a crocodile meal. The story went from one adventure to another deep into the interior of New Guinea.

As we bid each other good night, Joe seemed like he was recalculating the no-action part of his theory for those who followed God. No doubt he replayed a few of the scenes from the stories in his mind as he drifted off to sleep that night; after all, his fortress probably could not withstand a direct attack from a wayward crocodile lost on his part of the lawn.

Poor Joe, he could not have had his theories more completely discredited and thoroughly challenged. Blain continued to tell of experiences in Russia, of other answers to prayer. His life had been filled with one adventure after another since he had surrendered his life to God's plan. God had arranged the circumstances and testimonies. Each one had spoken directly to an issue challenging Joe's heart. Every question seemed to have been met with an answer. Through all the experiences shared, God was preparing Joe for a personal experience he would never forget.

It was the last day of our time at the mission and we needed to completely reframe the roof on the girls' dormitory and cafeteria. We calculated that with all of us working together we would be able to complete the enormous task before leaving the next day.

The sun rose in a cloudless sky with a vengeance that became unbearable. It was only mid morning with temperatures nearing one hundred degrees. We tried to press on, knowing how important it would be to those we left behind to have their roof rebuilt before the SOS team had to return home. By noon we were overcome with heat exhaustion. It was so unmercifully hot our bodies were reeling. We were blinded by sweat. Further progress was impossible. We were left with no other choice but to surrender our work on the roof, retreating to the nearby shade. We waited helplessly, looking at each other, unable to make another move. We knew that unless God worked a miracle we would be unable to complete the work that so badly needed to be finished.

We weakly formed a circle and began to pray. "Lord, we need Your help. We have come to serve You and bless these dear people, but we are helpless in this heat. Please, Lord, make it possible for us to finish this work if it will glorify Your name. In the name of Jesus we pray, amen." We opened our eyes, feeling the presence of God.

We waited only a moment or two before someone happened to look up to the sky above the small mountains cradling the mission. "Look over there! Look at the sky over that mountain;

there are clouds coming," he exclaimed with enthusiasm. It was an awe-inspiring moment, watching a thick covering of clouds being drawn across the cloudless sky like a giant canopy. We knew we were a part of a divine drama being enacted before our eyes. Within minutes we stood looking at a complete cloud covering in the sky with temperatures dropping steadily. We were not only refreshed by the coolness, we were inspired by a God who had not forgotten our names and had heard our cry for help. We felt His nearness surround us. We moved into action, working at double our previous pace. It was just about dusk when we climbed down from the roof of the completed building.

Joe had just experienced the amazing miracle that God had planed for him when He called his name a couple weeks earlier. His entire attitude had changed story by story, day by day. God's final move had inspired all of us with a new sense of His love and care for those who call upon Him in the day of trouble.

As we drove away from the mission, it was with a sense of accomplishment and wonder at the providence of God. Truly, God had demonstrated once again that He knows our names.

Joe had escaped every savory root served at mealtime. Not one of those tempting tubers, (purple potatoes as Joe called them) had managed to grace his lips during our entire stay. On the other hand, it seemed that nothing other than the array of tubers had passed mine. As I thought about how hungry I was just for a slice of bread, I reminded myself that I was the one leaving, but those who stayed would continue to be hungry for bread. I still wasn't sure if it had been coveting to look longingly at Joe's stash in his suitcase-grocery store. It did help to know that Joe had eaten all but the lining of his suitcase. I no longer needed to picture the tempting display that had once been treasured inside.

It seemed to be an appropriate stop for a night at an all-inclusive hotel on the Caribbean Sea before returning home. Joe had little trouble transitioning to the swimming pool, buffet, and all the tropical drinks he could drink. I believe Joe broke every record for drinking pina coladas. Surely, a new record was set. He stood for hours in waist-deep water of the swimming pool under the tropical sun with his arm outstretched, waiting for the man in the white jacket to grace his palm with yet another one of those rich white creamy drinks. I fear that the Dominican Republic lost an entire coconut grove and a small pineapple plantation to Joe's outstretched arm. He looked more like an Italian statue with a grinning white mustache than a young man who was supposed to be swimming in a pool. It was a wonderful conclusion to a week of miracles.

If the Creator of the vast universe filled with planets and stars called Joe's name at the precise moment he was trying to run from Him, don't you think He knows your name as well?

JAVIER

—◦«(●)»◦—

Javier sat up with a start as the boom from a loud blast of thunder rattled the glass in the window beside his bed. "What was that?" he wondered, rubbing the sleep from eyes opened wide in fear. Four-year-old Javier clutched his blanket, trying to be brave. As the next bolt of lightning lit his room, bravery gave way to terror. At the top of his lungs, Javier proclaimed his fear.

In an instant his mother was at his bedside. Holding her terrified little boy in her arms she said, "It's OK Javier. I am here now. You are safe." The lightning continued to flash bright beams of light throughout the room. Deafening claps of thunder followed each burst of light, causing the whole house to shudder from the mighty force. Heavy raindrops pelted the window, accenting the demonstration of nature's power. In the safety of his mother's arms, Javier's loud sobs quieted. The cascade of tears ceased their flow. With moistened cheeks pressed close to his mother's side, Javier felt safe once again. "Javier, you don't need to be afraid of thunder. It is God bowling up in heaven," his mother began. "Look at all those rain drops hitting the window. Do you know where they come from? Those are God's tears. He is crying because of all the sin and pain in our world," his mother explained.

Javier's mother understood very little about the God described in the Bible. She was simply sharing the only comfort she knew. As a little girl in Puerto Rico, her mother had calmed her fears of lightning and thunder with this simple explanation. From time to time she attended church with her parents, never really understanding much about God. He remained a mystery. She was sure of one thing—she wanted her children to know He was watching over all that happens on earth.

Javier's eyes became heavy in the safety of his mother's arms. Her soothing words comforted him as the storm moved into the distance. Tucked under the covers Javier blinked his eyes a couple of times before returning to the peaceful dream world of a four-year-old.

Javier's mother worked tirelessly from morning till night to make her home feel special for her family. Although she tried her best to make Javier, his younger brother, and three older sisters feel the warmth and love that she desired, it was not always easy. His father would often stop at the bar on his way home from work. When he came home, love for his wife and children were not foremost on his mind or lips. His greetings were at times like sharp arrows wounding everyone in the family. Arguments between Javier's parents became more and more frequent as he grew older. The tension continued to grow year after year. As he entered his teens, his mother could endure no more. Javier's father was invited to take his abusive, hurtful words elsewhere. She would make it on her own if need be. Her children were not going to grow up under a cloud of constant fighting and arguing.

After a few months of separation, Javier's father began calling home, desiring to be reunited with his family. He met some people who had introduced him to a whole new way of life. His evenings were now spent in Bible study. He was a new man. No longer did he feel the need to stop at the bar on his way home from work. Over and over he pleaded for the opportunity to come home. He would be a husband and father this time. His home would be different, he promised.

After a few months of earnest entreaty, permission was granted for Javier's father to return. Javier was not so sure he was glad his father was back. He was constantly talking about God and the Bible. "I don't think I like my dad this way any better than before," Javier said to himself. The more he thought about it, the more frustrated and angry he became. "We don't need some new religion crammed down our throat. Our religion is just fine. I don't like all these people coming over to our house with their Bibles, either." Javier, now a teenager, desired independence. New lists of rules and regulations were not welcome. Feelings of anger and resentment toward his father began to resurface. Years of abusive pain left many wounds deep inside.

Javier no longer looked forward to weekends. His father was insistent that everyone was going to his new church. One morning as the family was getting dressed for church, Javier decided he was not going to be forced to go. "I am not going to that dumb church any more," Javier announced to his father.

"You will do as you are told, young man," his father angrily shouted back.

"You think you can come back here strutting your holy stuff, and we are all just supposed to hop to. Well, I for one am done with your religion!" Javier replied defiantly.

From various vantage points the family observed the showdown. Enraged by Javier's defiance, his father looked him in the eye and declared his final ultimatum, "Javier, either you get dressed right now and get in the car with us, or get your things and get out!"

Feeling like a bomb about ready to explode, Javier opened his mouth to make his bid for departure. Opening his mouth to speak, a small movement from the kitchen caught his eye. Looking past his enraged father, he saw his mother's eyes silently pleading for him not to leave. Seeing the love in her eyes he knew it would break her heart if he walked away. Javier stood motionless between the anger radiating from his father's face and the love in his mother's pleading eyes. Not wanting to wound her heart, he turned slowly toward the bedroom to change his clothes.

Arriving at church, Javier's feelings of anger were just beneath the surface. "He can make me come to church, but he can't make me do all the dumb stuff these kids do here," Javier muttered under his breath as he shuffled to the door. Spotting a couple of other kids he knew would be up for a good challenge; he invited his comrades to assist him in disrupting the youth program at opportune moments. By the end of the service the youth leaders were very thankful to end the session. Being mocked and called dorky, laughed at and ridiculed, had not been all that pleasant. Javier and his buddies were informed their little sideshow had not been appreciated. Each week as he returned to church, feelings of forced religion sparked resentment and anger. Each week the youth leaders reminded him that his behavior was not appreciated.

Javier groaned as his father informed the family that they would be going to church on a weeknight for some special meetings held by a visiting speaker. Annoyed and disgruntled, he shuffled his way to the family car. "What are we doing at church in the middle of the week," he muttered as they pulled into the church parking lot. One side of the sanctuary was partially filled as Javier's family entered. Making sure all in attendance understood his position of protest, he made his way to the opposite side of the church, slouching in a pew by himself.

The visiting pastor began his presentation enthusiastically proclaiming, "This world belongs to Satan." For the next several minutes he reinforced his theme. In conclusion, and making certain that no one had missed his point, he looked out at the audience declaring, "If you choose this world, you too will belong to Satan." Turning from his audience, he faced the lone listener slouched in his pew. With his finger pointing straight at Javier he said, "Javier, if you choose this world, you will belong to Satan." Every eye turned in the direction of the pastor's pointed finger.

Javier felt like he would explode. His emotions and feelings of outrage could not be contained. Who did this visiting pastor think he was? How dare he be so cold and heartless! He had just been singled out before the entire congregation! Like a bursting volcano erupting with lava, he leaped to his feet. He knew that this man did not even know him. The church members had no doubt tipped off the one who had publicly rebuked him. In rage, he lunged for a vacant chair near by, intending to send it directly in the direction of the outstretched finger pointing at him. As he grabbed the chair with both hands, preparing to send it as an airborne message to the visiting preacher, he glanced in the direction of his parents seated across the aisle.

His eyes met the pleading, loving eyes of his mother saying, "Javier, please don't do it." The power in those eyes once again stayed his feelings of anger and rage. Pushing the chair from him, Javier faced his father shouting, "Don't you ever ask me to come to this church again!" With every eye riveted upon him, Javier stormed out.

Javier's father could see that forcing his son to go to church simply would not work any longer. Envisioning chairs sailing through the air across the sanctuary at visiting pastors sufficiently impressed him not to press the issue further. The anger and resentment he had been harboring in his heart since childhood refused to remain silent anymore. With each passing year his feelings of rebellion became more and more obvious.

By the time Javier finished high school he had learned well how to survive in the streets. He and his friends spent most of their time using and selling drugs. Their lifestyle brought them in constant contact with gangs. Living life outside the law placed Javier and his friends in one dangerous situation after another. It did not take long to discover that in the underworld, criminals write their own rules. A person's life was cheap in the dark culture he had chosen. His life was no exception. As a result of a business deal gone sour, a contract was placed on his life. Miraculously, he eluded his sentence. On several other occasions Javier's life was spared. Many of Javier's friends were not as fortunate. Some were killed; others went to prison. The life he thought would lead to excitement and freedom had become just the opposite. He was running from a God who would not let him go. Repeatedly he heard the loving voice of God inviting him to return to true freedom and happiness. Stubbornly refusing, he continued to drift further and further away.

The only way Javier could quiet his troubled soul was to deny the existence of the One who continued to call to him. Telling himself repeatedly "There is no God," he continued his course.

The ringing telephone interrupted Javier's half-hearted gaze in the direction of the television one sunny afternoon. "Javier, let's go down to the club and hang out for awhile. I'll stop by and pick you up in a few minutes," suggested his cousin. Javier and his cousin had become real soul mates. They hung out together most of the time. Having someone watching your back was more than just a good idea. It had proven to be the difference between life and death more than once. Walking into the club they spotted several friends who had also come in search of a good time. Finding a couple of empty seats at one of the tables they joined the party. The next couple of hours were spent like so many other visits to the club, drinking away painful realities. Like the majority surrounding them, they were desperately trying to discover the meaning of happiness. Each attempt left them feeling emptier than the last. Deciding it was time to leave, Javier and his cousin walked to the door.

"Where to now, Javier?" his cousin asked as they began to walk to their car.

Before Javier had time to reply, one of their friends came running up to them, asking for some backup in a street fight that was about to start. "Javier, it looks like we are going to have to throw down with those guys over there. They are giving us a little trouble," Javier's cousin called over his shoulder as he started walking rapidly in the direction of his waiting friends.

Javier turned to size up the situation. It looked like it would be a real rumble as the rivals began to face off. Taking a step forward, Javier felt an invisible, powerful force turn him sharply to the right. He was being held fast by an unseen power. At the same moment he felt his body being turned, his eyes focused intently upon a bottle that was being picked up by an angry young man a few feet away. Unable to move, he stood transfixed as the bottle was thrown directly toward his face. Suddenly the whole world felt as if it were in slow motion. With a feeling of helplessness, he watched the bottle come sailing directly at his face.

His instinct screamed from within, "Duck, Javier! Duck!" But he was frozen in his tracks with his eyes riveted on the bottle that was about to impact with violent force. Unable to make an effort to dodge the bottle, his thoughts screamed out, "I'm finished! I'm through!" The bottle came within inches of his face, stopped in mid air, and then fell to the ground. In amazement, Javier stood staring at the broken bottle at his feet.

At that instant he felt a strange sensation of love and warmth surrounding him. He could feel he was not alone. Transfixed, he heard a voice say, "Javier, I have something better for you. It is time for you to leave all this behind. This does not make you happy. What I have for you is better than anything you have ever experienced in your life!"

Javier was frozen in his tracks in the presence of an unseen being. He realized that God had just spoken personally to him. Just as quickly as the slow motion experience came, it ended. Feeling like he had just stepped back in time from a trip in an unreal world, he looked over at his cousin in action. He knew he had to leave. Contemplating what had just taken place with the words of invitation to a better life echoing throughout his consciousness left him visibly shaken. Running over to his cousin, he grabbed him by the shoulders just as he was about to take another swing.

"We've got to get out of here. Something has happened. Come on, we've got to go," Javier pleaded.

With one last look in the direction of the angry, fighting mob, they turned to make their escape. Never before had either of them walked away from a fight. This unexplainable retreat was a baffling mystery. "Javier, what is going on?" his cousin asked breathlessly as they ran toward their car.

"I'll tell you in a minute. Let's just get out of here," Javier called over his shoulder. Once in the car, Javier tried to explain the supernatural encounter he had just experienced, but it all seemed too unreal. His most vivid attempts met with stares of disbelief. "What's gotten into the Javier I thought I knew so well?" wondered Javier's cousin. As they drove, Javier repeatedly tried to make him understand, but it was no use. It all seemed like a fantastic dream.

From that day on, Javier's life slowly began to change. It was not an immediate transformation, but now he knew for himself God was real. He had to find out more about a God who would bother with someone like himself. Finding a Bible, Javier held it sacredly, staring at the book that supposedly communicated to human beings. Holding the Bible, Javier began his first real prayer to God. "God, I am going to read Your Bible, and I need You to talk to me. Now I know You are real! Please speak to me as I read from these pages."

Not knowing what to expect or where to start, Javier carefully opened the Bible, seeking an encounter with God. The more he read, the more he desired to read. Each time he invited God to speak to him personally through His Word. Often he discovered passages that felt they had been included just for him. He knew God had heard and answered his prayer, preserving special promises in His Word just for him. Reading the Bible became an adventure he didn't want to miss.

At work one day, Javier met two older men who enjoyed talking about God. In the evenings Javier began to study the Bible with Wilber and Frank. The knowledge of these two Christian men quickly won Javier's confidence as well as his heart. One day Wilbur said, "Javier, I know you would really enjoy something that will be starting soon at our church. We will be a host site for a satellite evangelistic crusade entitled Net 95. A pastor named Mark Finley will be speaking to people around the world from one location beamed up to satellite. You would learn many new things about prophecy and the Bible. You won't want to miss it."

Night after night Javier joined Wilbur and Frank at the meetings. As he learned more and more of God's love for him, the more convicted he became that God was inviting him to surrender his life. As the Spirit of God surrounded him, he promised God, no more clubs, no more drinking, no more drugs. Each day his experience grew deeper.

At the close of one of the meetings, an invitation was given to surrender all to Jesus. Quietly Javier sat contemplating all that God had done for him and the numerous times He had spared his life. He pondered the many times God had spoken to him with His still small voice.

"Lord, I want to give You my whole life. I want You to change all of me. Please help me," Javier prayed. A sense of God's peace filled his soul as he made his surrender to God.

The final meeting was drawing to a close. Javier hated to see the meetings end. He had learned so many new things. At the end of the meeting, the pastor invited all who would like to make a full surrender to Jesus in baptism to come forward. Javier wrestled within himself as people began to make their way to the front. Should he go forward for baptism? The pastor continued his invitation. For those desiring to make a full surrender to Jesus there would be a special prayer of dedication.

Quietly Javier slipped to his knees from the pew he was sitting on. "Lord, I am not going forward because a man says to go, but if You want me to go, I'll go. I want to give You everything. Just show me what to do," he prayed. With his eyes still closed, a bright beam of light descended on him, surrounding him in an overpowering atmosphere of light and love. Overcome with God's response to his prayer, he rose and with a beaming smile, made his way to the front of the church to join those making a full surrender to Jesus. Overwhelmed with God's love, Javier shared his sentiments with the congregation as he walked forward. "God loves you all. I feel so happy! Jesus is telling me to tell you that He loves you," Javier boldly proclaimed to those he was joining in the front.

Every eye was now on the last one making his way to the front, loudly proclaiming God's love as he walked. Javier felt foolish as he hugged one after another of those standing with him in the front of the church. "People are going to think I am crazy, but I just can't stop," he thought. "God just told me to get baptized. I am going to get baptized!" he jubilantly proclaimed. Javier spotted two of his friends who he had known from his party life standing in the group. With his face aglow he slipped in beside them.

The beam of light that had descended upon Javier continued to flood his soul with the assurance of love and acceptance. As Javier entered the water to join the pastor, he knew he had found the meaning of true freedom. Stepping up out of the water Javier rejoined his friends. They also were enjoying the new freedom of surrender. With his face aglow, Javier opened his mouth and the words, "I am going to be a pastor," just came tumbling out!

"No way, dude! You are not going to be a pastor. What are you talking about?" responded his two bewildered friends. Vivid memories of the one who had just proclaimed his call to the ministry made his bold announcement a bit more than they could swallow.

Feeling embarrassed and surprised at the same time, Javier silently repeated their sentiments to himself, "What am I talking about? Where did that crazy idea come from? No way am I going to be a pastor." Feeling awkward, Javier bade his friends farewell and headed for home. "Whatever made me make such a foolish statement?" he wondered. He had a good job and was getting ready to buy a house; becoming a pastor certainly was not in his plan. He simply could not believe the words that had just come out of his mouth.

Javier lay down to go to sleep that night, but sleep would not come. He tossed and turned hour after hour with his words ringing in his ears. He could tell that God was near and not allowing him to sleep. "God, just let me go. I am doing OK. I have a good job, and I'm doing fine. Just leave me alone," Javier said as he wrestled with God. Night after sleepless night the battle continued. "Lord, I have a good job and I am making money. I am getting ready to buy a house. I am good now. What else do You want from me?" continued Javier's argument with God. Weary of his many nights of striving with God, Javier called Wilbur for advice.

After hearing of Javier's nightly encounters with God, Wilbur said, "Javier, I think God is telling you to go back to school to get a Christian education and be trained as a pastor."

"No way, Wilbur. You know me. I am no pastor," Javier replied. Talking to Wilbur certainly had been little consolation. His struggle continued another night. Another night of conflict resulted in another call to Wilbur.

Wilbur's position remained the same: "God is calling you to get a Christian education in preparation for the ministry."

Looking through a stack of bills one day, Javier came upon a half-completed application form for a Christian university. "That looks like my handwriting," he thought as he picked up the form, taking a closer look. He stared in amazement. It was his handwriting, but he had never seen this document before in his life. Quickly fumbling through some papers, he found another form with his handwriting to use as a comparison. It was a perfect match. Staring down at the form, Javier said in disbelief, "This is definitely me, but no way did I fill it out." Looking upward, Javier said, "OK God, I am done fighting You. I am going to fill out this application, but I know there is no way they will accept it."

Javier felt he was totally safe in his agreement with God since he had finished high school with a low D average. School had not been his first or even a close second in his priorities. Dropping his application in the mailbox, Javier looked at the large envelope, and with a smile and a challenge for God said, "Let's see how powerful You are now!"

A few days later a representative from the university called to speak with Javier about his application. Javier smiled as she informed him that his GPA was too low. "You would need at least three more credits to enroll," she continued.

Javier's mind raced. He was not off the hook yet. "A few months ago I stopped and enrolled in a class at a community college," Javier began. "I didn't know at the time why I stopped or what class I wanted to take, but when the registrar suggested a sociology class with three credits, I agreed. I recently completed the class. I didn't have a clue why I took it," Javier concluded. Shocked at what was developing, he informed the administrator that he indeed had the three needed credits. Within a few weeks he began his education. He was training to become a worker for God. Once again he was filled with amazement as he contemplated this most recent demonstration of God's leading and providence,

Javier completed his education by God's grace. Truly, God had called one of the most unlikely persons to work for him. He was now a pastor! God did not stop working miracles for Javier the day he became a pastor. He was just beginning. Pastor Javier Quiles is now in full-time ministry and evangelism. By the same power that fell upon him in that beam of light from heaven so many years ago, he has seen hundreds of young people surrender their lives to Jesus. God has taken him to places he never would have dreamed of, speaking many places in North America and occasionally internationally. God truly had something better in store for his life the day He invited him to leave his old life and follow Him.

If you were to ask Javier what one of the most significant moments in ministry has been, he would not hesitate to tell you. Leading his own mother to a complete surrender to Jesus and a decision for baptism was the most exciting of all. Holding his hand over his mother's head, baptizing her in the name of the Father, the Son, and the Holy Ghost, his joy could not be contained. Tears of joy spilled out, running down his cheeks.

If the Creator of the vast universe filled with planets and stars interrupted His affairs to call a young man, angry and in rebellion, don't you think He knows your name as well?

JORDAN

———)((0))(———

Looking into the eyes of His disciples Jesus said, "Except ye be converted, and become as little children, ye shall not enter into the kingdom of heaven." Simple, childlike faith was refreshing to Jesus' soul. No wonder He instructed His disciples, "Suffer the little children to come unto me, and forbid them not: for of such is the kingdom of God" (Mark 10:14). Children are as refreshing today as they were when Jesus walked among us. It is not the adults who think of bringing an umbrella to the special prayer meeting for rain; it is the child planning for a real cloud-burst. Reading Jordan's story will no doubt inspire you to look heavenward with a simple prayer, "Lord, help me to have a heart of faith just like Jordan."

Jordan was four years old. Growing up with a single mom struggling to make ends meet provided more than one challenge. Every day his mother would have an additional problem to solve that appeared to be without solution. Jordan learned early how to pray. He and his mother would often look heavenward, seeking God's help. Jordan loved going to church with Sasha, his mother. He especially enjoyed the activities, songs, and stories planned for young worshipers like himself. He practiced the new memory text each week with his mother so he could recite it without prompting in class the following week. He once learned an abbreviated version of the Ten Commandments so well that Pastor Steve, Jordan's buddy, invited him to come to the front of the church just prior to the worship hour to share his accomplishment with the congregation. By age four Jordan had already developed a simple childlike faith. He loved to listen to stories of Bible heroes in his books entitled *My Bible Friends*.

Jordan was not a saint by any means. He had a creative imagination that kept his mother on her toes every minute. He loved adventure and anything active. He once watched a video of a daring rescue and so completely identified with the hero that for weeks he proudly announced to every visitor that he was a rescue hero. Jordan paid very close attention to the details in the video. Certain protective articles are considered essential to all rescue heroes as they repeatedly place their lives on the line. After joining this elite group of daring public servants, Jordan could be observed with hard hat, safety goggles, and other apparel that would protect him from the dangers that threaten rescue heroes. In full protective gear and with the understanding that one must always expect the unexpected, he diligently searched the house over and over for anyone who might have become lost or seriously wounded. If detected, they would no doubt need to be rescued.

All who visited Jordan's home knew they could rest assured that their safety was secure as long as Jordan was on duty. At times Jordan's entire neighborhood could rest a little easier as they observed Jordan patrolling areas that only a rescue hero would be able to identify as potentially dangerous. At times, persons who previously had considered themselves in safe environments realized that their life had been spared unawares after a brief period of interrogation. The city of Columbus, Wisconsin would no doubt have saluted one of its bravest citizens had they been aware of the countless hours of selfless service invested by one of their young public servants. As you can see, Jordan was a very normal boy, with a creative imagination. Jordan was also a young Christian who had been introduced to Jesus and had accepted Him as an ever-present friend.

Fall comes early in Wisconsin, announcing the weather soon to come that in every way qualifies for the term winter. Temperatures had been steadily dropping with December just around the corner. Icy, howling winds had removed the last of the leaves from the trees, as a reminder that snow would soon follow. Money had been especially scarce for the past several weeks. Piggy banks had been empty for several days. Now every remaining penny counted. When the phone rang requesting Sasha's assistance as a baby sitter for the evening for a friend in a nearby town she readily agreed.

Donning their coats and hats, Sasha and Jordan jumped into the car for the short trip to their friend's home. Sasha glanced down at the gas gauge as she started the car. The haunting realization that their gas tank was empty and they very possibly would not make it the ten miles to the neighboring town glared back at her. The needle rested below the empty mark. She tried not to worry Jordan with the possibility of being stranded along the road in the blustery conditions. She knew with the money she would earn she would be able to put a few dollars' worth of gas in her tank and still have a precious dollar or two for other needs just as urgent. "If we can just make it to Amy's house we will be OK," Sasha reasoned. She really had no choice but to take off, hoping that the needle on her gas gauge was mistaken.

The car was cold, but there definitely was not gas enough for the desired pre-warming of the engine. Sasha tried to act unconcerned as they drove down the highway. Each mile marker they passed inched them just a little closer to the safety of Amy's warm home and the much-needed income. At last the final mile marker came into view. Just when it seemed they might make it, the engine sputtered and died. Coasting off the highway to a frontage road, the car came to complete stop.

"What's wrong with the car, Mom?" Jordan asked.

"Our car doesn't have any more gas in the tank, so the motor stopped," Sasha replied.

"How long will we have to sit here before someone comes to help us, Mom? Will it get as cold in the car as it is outside?"

"Jordan, I don't know. We will just have to wait for a little while and see what happens," Sasha said with a prayer in her heart. As she looked around, she noticed the car had stopped almost directly in front of a steep hill with a road descending directly to where their car had died. This looked like it could be very dangerous. With conditions well below freezing, someone might come sliding down the hill and come crashing into the side of their helplessly stranded car.

Silent prayers continued to flow heavenward for wisdom. Over and over Sasha turned the key in the ignition without even a sputter. It was no use—cars simply don't run without gas. She was certainly thankful for the cell phone in her pocket. She dialed Amy's number, hoping she would not get a busy signal. "Why isn't she answering the phone? She has to be home. She is expecting me any minute to come and watch her children," Sasha said nervously to herself.

Jordan continued to ask the how long and why questions that could not be answered. The reality of the situation seemed to be more and more serious by the moment. What should they do? After some moments of silence Jordan said, "Mom, why don't we pray?"

Feeling a little frustrated Sasha said, "OK, Jordan, why don't you pray?"

"Dear Jesus," Jordan began, "our car is out of gas and we don't want someone to crash into us. Would You help us start our car? Amen."

They raised their heads, looking around to see if anyone had come to their rescue, but not a soul was in sight. After a long moment of silence Jordan turned to his mother and said, "Well, aren't you going to start the car?"

Sasha's mind raced. Now what should she do? She did not want to diminish Jordan's simple faith. She thought of telling him that sometimes God doesn't answer our prayers right away, but that just did not seem like it would help at the moment. There must be a better answer. What could she say that would not somehow cause Jordan's friendship with God to be challenged?

Jordan repeated his previous request with a bit more urgency. "Mom, come on. Turn the key and start the car."

Sasha knew she could not avoid the dreaded moment any longer. She had to at least turn the key for Jordan. "Well, here goes. I'll have to just turn it and then try to think of what to say to him after nothing happens," she thought as she slowly turned the key. She knew she would soon face another series of why-didn't-God-answer-my-prayer questions when nothing happened. Suddenly, the motor roared to life as if the tank was completely full. Sasha was stunned. She quickly put the car in drive and moved out of harm's way. As soon as the car was out of danger from the hillside intersection, the car died once again.

Looking up at his mother Jordan simply stated, "I knew Jesus would start our car."

Sasha sat in silence as she sensed the presence of God and His gentle voice reminding her that He would always be there for her.

"You need to learn to trust Me, just like Jordan. I will never leave you or forsake you," came the still, small voice.

"Please forgive me Lord, for my lack of faith," Sasha silently prayed.

Within a few minutes an earlier call home to Mom was rewarded with a can of gas, and the rejoicing duo were on their way to the warm home waiting just ahead.

Does God know the name of even a small child? If you are in doubt, check with Jordan. He will be able to assist you with the answer.

If the Creator of the vast universe filled with planets and stars would answer the faint cry from a small boy, don't you think He knows your name as well?

MARC

arc is an inmate in a maximum-security prison, serving a seventy-five-year sentence.

I first met Marc as he completed the tenth year of his sentence at age thirty-two. He was searching for a friend, someone who really cared. His hurting heart longed for someone to be genuine. Every family member except his mother had rejected and distanced themselves from him. Even her relationship was somewhat strained as she attempted to interact intermittently with her son. Marc felt about as self-condemned, rejected, and ostracized as a person could feel. Lesa and I repeatedly had the privilege of visiting him. As might be expected, he had inherited a very distorted view of God. We prayed that God would use us to paint a new picture of Himself to one so desperately in need. I believe it will be useful for anyone feeling that God perhaps knows the names of the good people on planet earth, but aren't so sure about those who know they don't qualify for His list of most obedient, to hear a portion of Marc's story.

Marc grew up in a sad, dysfunctional home where abuse had been perpetrated for several generations. At an early age he became a victim of pain and abuse that characterized not only his immediate family, but relatives as well. By the time he began his adolescent years he had been so repeatedly abused he had little concept of what the term love meant.

At this critical period in his life his father opted to move on, leaving his mother to try her best on her own. It was not a sad day for Marc to see one of his chief offenders move out of the house. It would mean no more pain from the one who should have been his protector and friend; it would also mean they would have no idea where their food would come from.

Marc's mother took a factory job, leaving him alone in a big city after school. Marc soon discovered that many other boys his age lacked fathers. Together they learned how to make it in the asphalt jungle. Early in life they learned they could numb the pain as they experimented with drugs and alcohol. It didn't take long for this to become his lifestyle.

Mark married young, without a clue what it meant to be a husband or a father. His home deteriorated quickly. His wife became disillusioned with what she had hoped would be a happy home. After only a few years of marriage Marc was convicted of a series of serious crimes. When the facts were presented to the judge, and a review of his case completed, Marc was given the maximum sentence—seventy-five years.

Learning some of Marc's story, I decided to write him a short letter, offering to visit him. He had experienced more than one disappointing visit and was not sure he wanted another stranger coming to straighten him out. We had just returned from a mission trip to Central America. Looking over her recently developed photos, Lesa felt impressed to send the duplicates to Marc. Perhaps the colorful pictures in a tropical setting would be meaningful to someone in prison. Each photo had a personal note on the back to explain its context. With a prayer, Lesa mailed Marc her little package of mission pictures. The photos touched Marc's heart with a feeling that someone did care after all. His cell became a connection to the outside as most of the inmates in his cellblock came for a little travelogue with Lesa's photos. Marc so enjoyed seeing the beauty of the outdoors, as well as places he had never had the opportunity to visit before, that we made it a point from then on to always bring back either postcards or photos when traveling. With photos in hand, Marc sent us a letter of invitation to visit him and added our names to his visitors list.

The series of disasters defining the life of a boy who had never known what it was to live a day of safety and peace, characterized the man sitting across from us in the visiting room of the prison. Marc was an intelligent man with eyes that carefully studied the expression and body language of visitors. He quickly determined a person's genuineness. People visiting prison either reach out a caring hand of love and friendship, or are just superficial do-gooders trying to make themselves feel good by visiting someone in prison.

One morning as Lesa was praying and reading her Bible, she asked the Lord, "Is there someone special that You would have me pray for today?" Almost instantly Marc's name came to mind. "Lord, please be with Marc today in a special way," Lesa began. "May he be aware of Your presence all day today. Bless his life with the reality of Your presence. Lord, You know that Marc's heart is wounded and lonely. Please touch him in a way that will bring healing to his life. As I think of Marc's sad life, I don't think he has ever known or experienced real joy or happiness even one of those days. I ask You for a special blessing of joy to fill Marc's life today so he will know You are letting him experience Your joy, the joy of the Lord." As Lesa's heart began to feel the sadness Marc must have experienced in his life, she continued to talk with God. "Let him experience the kind of joy that the psalmist describes as the fullness of joy from being in Your presence. I want to thank You in advance for the special gift You have planned today for Your son Marc." She then ended her prayer with, "I praise You and thank You Father, in Jesus' name. Amen."

As Lesa walked to work that day, she invited the Lord to impress her throughout the day to lift Marc up in prayer and ask for the gift of joy to keep surrounding him all day long. Many times that day Marc came to mind, and each time Lesa would lift him up in prayer. About the middle of the day, as Lesa ended a prayer for Marc, she felt a strong impression to write Marc a note letting him know that she had been asking God to give him a special gift of joy for the entire day.

A few days later, an interesting reply came in the mail. "Lesa, I want to tell you the amazing way that God answered your prayer!" Marc's letter began. "I had just come back from breakfast with my cellmate when our whole room seemed to fill with a most wonderful sensation, like nothing I had ever experienced before. I just started grinning from ear to ear. I felt so happy inside. I had never experienced anything remotely close to this in my life. From time to time someone would stop by for a moment and stare at my cellmate and me, just grinning in our cell. I wish I could find the words to tell you what all this felt like. It was so wonderful. We could tell that we were in the presence of the Lord, and it filled us with so much joy we could not believe it! The really amazing thing is this joyful experience lasted all day long, just like you prayed. Some of the other inmates were rather disgusted with my grinning continually at them and asked what my problem was and why I was so happy. I could only grin and say, 'I don't know!' Even the guards looked at us kind of funny as they checked on us, asking what we were so happy about. We didn't know what to say, so we just kept on smiling. They just shook their heads and walked away. We lay down to go to sleep that night with the same big grin still on our faces. When we woke up the next morning we both wondered what had happened the day before. A couple of days later I got your note. As I read it, it dawned on me what had happened just two days earlier, and I started smiling all over again. I can't wait for you to come for a visit so I can tell you about our day in person. Hope to see you soon."

Marc's letter was decorated with smiley faces, stars, sunbeams, and many other graphic art displays punctuating the beginning and ending of sentences.

Lesa opened the mail that evening after supper while I was working in the other room on the computer. As she read the wonderful way that God had answered her prayer, she was overjoyed. God had blessed Marc the very way she had requested, and the blessing had spilled over on his cellmate as well.

Lesa came hurrying into the room where I was working with the highly decorated letter in her hands. "Greg, listen to the way God answered my prayer for Marc," she said with a smile. Excitedly, she went from highlight to highlight, as I continued to focus on the computer. When she finished she said, "Isn't that exciting Greg?" Glancing in her direction and then back to the computer I said, "Uh, huh. That's nice." With a rather disgusted look on her face, she returned to the living room where she decided the only One to talk to about it would be the One who had just worked the wonderful miracle in response to her prayer.

Perhaps this would be a good place to insert a tip for men reading this story. I just scored a .01 on the well-known chart of 1–1000 used by wives to measure the listening skills of husbands. Scores nearing 1000 are considered to be in the good listening range, while .01 might not be considered all that impressive. A bit of advice that may be useful in the future: if you have any romantic thoughts that you are hoping will become a reality you may want to try to think of a more original response than "Uh huh." If you are reading the paper, watching the news, or polishing your golf clubs, and your wife approaches with the intent of opening her heart, an "uh huh; that's nice" response, while maintaining your focus upon your current task, will more than likely result in a low score. While I know of no scientific studies that can validate these findings, I have found the scoring and results to be fairly consistent.

Returning to the living room, Lesa sat on the floor and began praising the Lord for His wonderful answer to her prayer for Marc. In the midst of her reflection and praise, the thought of one of her daughters came to mind. All day she had been bombarded with discouragement because of the choices her daughter had been making. God chose this moment to speak a word of encouragement to Lesa, His daughter, weighed down with a spirit of heaviness for her own daughter.

In the quietness of the moment, God said to her, "You have seen what your prayers have done for Marc. Now guess what I can do with your prayers for your daughter?"

With God's gentle answer, the power of discouragement was broken and peace returned to Lesa's heart. God used Marc's letter as a means of speaking hope and encouragement to the one who had sent him a letter. It came on the very day she needed it most.

In a few days we made a visit to the prison to listen to Marc's personal account of his fullness-of-joy day. After a brief wait in the visiting room, Marc came walking across the room filled with inmates and family members with a smile across his face too big to miss. Sitting across from us, he began to recount his amazing day all over again. Marc had been waiting for our visit and for the opportunity to relive many of his experiences with us. The thought of the wonderful day and the blessings from being in God's presence filled him with such happiness that his countenance radiated with joy once again. We listened to him describe many of the experiences he had tried to describe in his letter.

After sharing many of his moments of joy and happiness, he paused with a focused look on his face saying, "I have been waiting to tell you one other experience that became one of the most unforgettable of the day. In the wonderful atmosphere of God's presence, my cellmate and I felt impressed to open the Bible and begin reading various passages. After a while we turned to the gospel of John. We continued reading and listening to words that seemed to be speaking personally to us. After we finished reading John chapter 13, detailing the Last Supper in the upper room, we paused for a moment of reflection. The whole picture was so moving. I asked my cellmate if I could wash his feet like Jesus had done for the disciples. Neither of us had ever witnessed anything like this before, but we could feel the Spirit directing and leading us through an experience that Jesus had outlined for His disciples, telling them that happiness would follow as they washed one another's feet." Pausing for a moment, he looked at us with an inquisitive gaze, studying our response. He then asked us, "Have you ever heard of anything like this before?"

We assured him we had and that this ordinance of humility can truly be a cleansing experience for all who follow Jesus example. As our visiting time came to an end, we prayed quietly together, thanking God for His wonderful gifts of love for Marc and his cellmate.

In a few weeks we returned to the prison to visit Marc. He had another story for us. He began by telling us some of the ways his life had been changing as a result of his day with God. He felt like a new man with a different outlook on life. His job each day was to clean the floors in the discipline area of the prison known as the Hole. He described the life of those unfortunate enough to end up in this most undesirable place of solitary confinement. Most offenders need only one dose of this place to make necessary behavioral corrections. The isolation, no reading materials, and an altered menu in cramped quarters leaves a lasting impression.

Many of the convicts Marc encountered in this part of the prison were really only kids. They had become involved with gangs, committed terrible crimes, and were given sentences to match. Many seventeen and eighteen year olds down in the Hole were trying to process two-hundred-year sentences that were attached to their name and number. They came from homes that really weren't homes at all, without a dad, and sometimes with multiple combinations of people trying to exist together in small quarters. Their hearts were further wounded as they lived out their pain by fighting and killing in the streets. The judges, on the other hand, not wanting to appear soft on crime, maximized the sentences of many of these kids to appear in control of their jurisdiction. Even Marc was trying to imagine what it must feel like to be seventeen with a two-hundred-year sentence. "These kids are so emotionally unbalanced, you would not believe it," concluded Marc.

One day while Marc cleaned the floors in this undesirable portion of the prison, he encountered one of these hurting young men. "As I came alongside the cell this young boy was in, he began screaming the most bizarre profanity. As you can imagine, living in a place like this we have heard about anything that could come out of a person's mouth. The words coming out of his mouth sounded like demons screaming from within. His words were the most vile and abominable that I had ever heard come from a human being.

"My first impulse was to respond with a similar discourse of my own, putting him in his place. Just before I went to open my mouth, I felt the presence of God come over me, filling me with compassion for this boy who was nearly insane with the painful reality that this would be his life until he died. I remembered the power of your prayer for me and felt moved to pray for God's Spirit to minister to this hurting heart as He had my own.

"Looking into the face of this young boy, I began to pray silently for God's power and grace to surround him. I prayed for healing to anoint the deep pain he had felt, probably his whole life. As I began to pray, the cursing froze in midstream. The young man just stared silently at me as I continued to pray silently for him. Both of us could tell something unusual was taking place, but only I knew what it was.

"After a few moments I moved down the hall, cleaning in a strange atmosphere of silence. I knew God had heard and answered my prayer just as He had for you. It was thrilling to experience the power of God working in the life of another because I had prayed." Marc ended his story just as our visiting time expired.

We made our way home contemplating the love of a God who knows no bounds, reaching into the very dregs of humanity with grace and mercy from His throne above.

If the Creator of the vast universe filled with planets and stars can hear the cry of a wounded criminal from the depths of a maximum security prison, don't you think He knows your name as well?

JIM

—=≫•《(●)》•≪=—

E arl Jennings' life began during the challenging years known
as the Depression in McAlester, Oklahoma. His father worked
hard, making just enough money for the bare necessities.
Life was a challenge, but they were making it. When Earl was just
one-and-a-half-years old, his father became terminally ill. Earl's
mother watched her husband slip away from her day by day. It
wasn't long until he closed his eyes, never to awaken again.

At this time the social services now in place were not available.
With her husband's extended illness, it had been some time since
there had been any income. Now she was alone. She had no one
to turn to for help. She looked into her baby boy's eyes and said,
"How will I ever take care of you?" Feeling the hopelessness of her
situation, she made a decision she never dreamed she could make.
She would have to send her children to an orphanage. Learning of
such a facility in Joplin, Missouri, she decided she had no choice
but to say goodbye to her children. She took comfort knowing they
would be cared for.

Earl's home became one of the little beds in the orphanage.
He lived the next year and a half with many other children longing for a loving touch. They wanted someone to make them feel
special. The place designed for love in Earl's heart could only wait

and hope that someone would want to adopt a little boy and call him their own.

When he was three years old, the Dixon family came to the orphanage in search of a little boy. Earl was chosen and adopted into their family. His new parents changed his name to Jim and took him home with them in Baxter Springs, Kansas. Jim longed for a loving touch now more than ever. He waited anxiously for a warm embrace from his new mother and father, but it never came. He could only look on as their love and affection was directed to their daughter, his new little sister.

Jim began to feel anger and resentment building up inside. He was given more and more chores to do while his sister played and enjoyed a normal childhood. His unhappiness, no doubt, contributed to the decision to send him, at age six, to work on an uncle's farm in Springdale, Arkansas. This uncle had no intentions of filling the empty hole in little Jim's heart. He had a long list of chores that would leave little time for a boy to wonder what to do.

A small room dug out of the dirt in the basement was his new bedroom. This new bedroom was little more than a cave built under the house that the rest of the family called home. It was impossible to keep clean living in the dirt and even more challenging to keep the dirt out of his simple bed. It was little consolation to a shivering little boy living under a house to know that everyone living above him was warm each night.

For three years Jim worked after school and from dawn until dark on the weekends. When Jim was ready for the third grade, his uncle decided he had had enough of him, and returned him to his home. After only two years at home his family decided they really didn't want him and sent him to work for another uncle in Kansas.

Jim was now in the fifth grade and was expected to work much like a hired man, only without pay. His uncle was a harsh man who would use his belt to beat him across his back if he did anything that displeased him. Poor Jim became so accustomed to the beatings that he scarcely responded with emotion. His anger grew day by day as he worked while the rest of the children played around the yard.

"Why am I being treated like this? What have I done that makes everyone feel like this about me? Will I never know what it feels like to be loved?" His mind could not sort out why his life was so filled with pain and disappointment.

One day several children came out to the farm to play with his sister. They laughed and played near the area that Jim was working in the hot sun. Finally Jim could stand it no longer and confronted his uncle with the injustice of his work while the others were having fun. He was told that the other children were guests at the farm, and if he knew what was good for him, he would get back to work.

As Jim worked near a small haystack, one of the boys playing in the yard ventured near. He could feel jealousy, anger, and a desire to lash out at someone rising to the surface as he called out a challenge. "Hey, Kenny, do think you are any match for king of the mountain?"

Kenny laughed as he snidely replied, "I could take you with one hand tied behind my back."

"Well come on then, if you aren't too chicken." With that the match was on. Jim positioned himself for the challenge.

The young boy had never encountered a boy his age having muscles like steel. Jim's muscles had been developing from dawn until dusk. The young visitor from the city immediately discovered he was no match for Jim. Jim's anger and resentment came flooding out against this poor, unsuspecting visitor. Within a few moments, he had managed not only to maintain his position as king of the mountain but had broken his challenger's arm. The boy screamed in pain as he ran for the house.

Jim knew what would be coming as punishment, but he didn't care anymore. He did not have long to wait as his uncle came running at him with his belt in hand. Poor Jim was beaten without mercy until his back was raw with welts and bruises. His heart became more and more empty and lonely the longer he lived without love.

When Jim was fourteen, he took a special liking to a horse that his uncle kept penned at all times. Ginger was a large, muscular horse that seemed to like Jim. He longed to ride his uncle's prize horse but was always told that Ginger was a killer horse that would throw her rider and then stomp him to death. He would walk near Ginger, talking to her and petting her whenever he could do so unobserved.

One evening Jim went to talk to Ginger. "Ginger, I don't think you are a killer horse. I think you would let me ride you, wouldn't you?" he said as he studied the eyes of the large horse. When the moon was high and all were asleep in the house upstairs, Jim crept out to the barn for his rendezvous with Ginger. Slipping the saddle over her back, he backed her up to a stall to climb on her tall back. "Ginger, remember! We are friends now. Be nice to me tonight and I will give you a chance to get out of your pen for some exercise," Jim soothingly said as they stepped into the moonlight pasture. It was freedom for both Jim and Ginger from a cruel taskmaster who had held them both hostage. For two hours, with the moon shining overhead, Ginger and Jim felt the breeze in their face. They felt as though they were floating on a cloud propelled by wings of freedom.

Jim and Ginger enjoyed their secret freedom seasons by night for several months. Time after time Jim pleaded with his uncle to let him have Ginger, but always with the same response, "Ginger is a killer, and you could never ride her." One day his uncle conceded to his request with a bargain for Ginger. "Jim, if you will work all the land and plant the crops after your regular chores are completed for the day, I will give Ginger to you," agreed his uncle.

For months Jim worked all day in the hot sun. Without a break he worked late into the night for the horse he loved. It was with a sense of real accomplishment that Jim looked over the farm as he completed the last day's work of the bargain. Turning from the field he headed back to the barn to claim his horse.

As he arrived at the gate Ginger was being loaded into another man's truck. "Hey!" Jim yelled. "What are you doing with my horse?"

His uncle turned and began to curse and swear at him, "This is not your horse, nor has it ever been your horse. I can do as I please with my horse."

With the cursing still lashing out at Jim, he just turned away knowing that he had been betrayed once again. It was not only the betrayal that stung. He had learned to genuinely love Ginger, and now she was going to someone else's farm.

After Ginger was gone, Jim told his uncle, "I will never work for you again."

Realizing this may be his last opportunity to teach Jim a lesson, his uncle beat him mercilessly. Jim packed his things and was sent back to his adopted parents in Baxter Springs. He couldn't help pondering the events of his life as he traveled. What had he done to be treated so unfairly? Bumping along the road Jim looked up and began to talk to the God he had heard was up there. A warm and loving voice reassured him that his cry had been heard. From that moment on Jim often paused to ask the God of heaven if He understood the pain of his heart.

No welcoming committee was awaiting Jim as he returned; instead, he was labeled as the boy who refused to work. In very plain language, his mother repeatedly informed him of her negative feelings for him. Feeling the rejection at home all over again, Jim spent as little time there as possible.

He soon met Johnny, another young man of fourteen. Johnny and Jim instantly became fast friends, learning to smoke, cuss, and once in a while sample some home brew together. Jim and Johnny began to plan the day they would leave town together. Jim told Johnny, "I know I will start fighting back any day now. I am tired of being beaten with the belt every time I turn around. If I don't get out of here soon, I will get myself into some real trouble."

Jim began to save every penny he could working at the theater and a newspaper route. After a few weeks he had enough money to buy an old car. He hid it out in a field near his house, covering it with branches and leaves. Each time he received a paycheck he bought canned goods and other nonperishable items, storing them in his car. Just a little longer and he would have enough food and cash for his getaway.

A few weeks later he decided he had enough to make his escape. Coming home one day, his mother greeted him at the door, informing him he should be out cleaning the barn.

"I just finished cleaning the barn," Jim replied.

"Then you should be raking the back yard," continued his mother.

"I finished raking yesterday," Jim said with a sad look on his face.

"Then you should be hoeing the garden," his mother said with an impatient tone to her voice.

"I have already hoed the garden. So what are you trying to say?" Jim asked.

"I want to get you out of this house any way I can. It wouldn't hurt my feelings one bit if you would just disappear," sneered his mother.

Broken and wounded again, Jim looked his mother in the eye and said, "In two or three days I will disappear."

His mother glared as she sneered some of the last words that Jim ever heard her say, "Jim, that would be the best news I have heard today."

He could only look heavenward telling his heavenly Father, "All I have ever wanted is to be loved. Is that too much to ask? I know I will never find it here. Lord, please be with me."

A couple of nights later Jim threw his things out the bedroom window and headed for his hidden car. As he walked to the car he looked heavenward, talking to God, "Lord, please be with me. I don't want to be alone." Uncovering his getaway car, Jim turned the key in the ignition and was on his way. Pulling up to Johnny's house, Jim went in to invite Johnny to accompany him on a trip that lacked any particular destination. Johnny's mother gave Jim a warm embrace, assuring him of her love as the two young men decided to head south to Johnny's sister's house in Texas. Adding a few of Johnny's belongings to the waiting car, the two boys were off.

Early in the morning two tired travelers pulled into Lubbock, Texas. Seeing a light come on in the house, Jim and Johnny climbed out of the car and went to the door to greet Johnny's sister and family. It was a joyous reunion for Johnny and his sister. As Johnny was hugged, kissed, and showered with affection, Jim stood behind watching. This demonstration of love was something he had longed to experience his whole life. The only one he could talk to was his unseen Father in heaven. He longed for just one person to include him in their circle of love. "Lord, what does it feel like to be touched like that? What does it feel like to be kissed? Will I ever know the kind of love Johnny is feeling right now?" prayed Jim.

As soon as the welcoming party ended, Johnny's sister headed directly to the kitchen calling over her shoulder, "You must be starved after such a long trip." The smells coming from the kitchen made the taste buds of the two young voyagers water in anticipation of a real meal. At last the table was set and Johnny's sister came in to call her family to a breakfast fit for a king. Everyone was warmly invited to the table; all, that is, but Jim.

"Johnny, you know we aren't about to feed your friends don't you? He can wait for you out in the back yard until you are finished eating."

Jim was shown to the back porch while the family laughed and exchanged pleasantries around the table. With breaking heart he could only look heavenward once again to talk to the one who had continually let him know He cared. "Lord, what about me? Will I always be the one in the way? Won't people ever care about me?" Jim sat thinking and talking to the dog lying on the back steps beside him. "Some friend Johnny is. I just drove him fourteen hundred miles. He shared my food. I paid for the gas. He rode in my car. And now he is enjoying a nice breakfast without a thought about me."

After several minutes Jim could hear the plates being cleared from the table and the clean-up process beginning. "Well, maybe there was a little left over, and they will think of sharing some with me," Jim thought. He was right. There were a few leftovers. The back door opened and Johnny came out with a large collection of food stacked high on a plate. Calling the resting dog sitting next to Jim, he filled his bowl to overflowing, turned, and walked back into the house.

Jim could not decide which hurt worse, his aching heart or his growling stomach. Half talking to the feasting dog and half to himself, he said, "It looks like I better drive to town and try to find some food."

Jim could see it was himself against the world once again. "I guess I will just have to find my own place in town," he mused as he drove along. Finding a little café, Jim ordered a small plate of food with some of the last of his money. Walking along the street he noticed an advertisement for a job at the bowling alley. With a little persistence Jim was soon working at the bowling alley at night and the town hotel by day. He found a very small trailer and, with a little negotiating, was able to call it his home. For the next few months Jim worked two jobs, trying to earn enough money to eat three times a day.

One day Johnny stopped by the hotel with a news flash he knew would interest Jim. "I heard your uncle has hired a detective to track you down. I guess he realized how much work you were doing, and isn't about to just let you go! I thought you might like to know."

Jim knew he had to go somewhere, but where? His new friend Bill had just the answer. "Let's go to Custer, South Dakota. I'll pay half the gas."

In a few moments the car was packed, and they were headed north. It was late fall as they arrived in Custer. Bill quickly located some family members to live with, leaving Jim alone. After asking around, Jim learned that the junkyard was looking for someone to remove parts from cars.

"I can't pay you much, but you can stay in that trailer out back if you want," offered the owner of the yard.

"I'll take it," Jim said.

As he opened the door to the little trailer he thought, "There is a reason this trailer is parked at a junk yard. This trailer is worse than the last one, but I guess I have no choice for now."

The hours were long, and the pay almost non existent. The mercury was steadily dropping night by night, sometimes falling to chill factors of -80 degrees. With no money for heat, Jim would dress in all his clothes, wrapping up as best he could. He spent night after night shivering until morning. Leaving his trailer each morning was like escaping from an icebox hotel.

After several days, Jim decided to venture into town. He was starving and penniless. Maybe he could find someone who would have compassion and give him a little food. Walking down the sidewalk he came to a restaurant. The window to the kitchen was open. A plate of steaming food heaped high waiting to be served rested on the sill. It was too much for Jim's starving stomach to endure.

"Lord, I promised that if You would be with me I would try to be good. You know how hungry I am right now. I am going to walk around the block. Please don't let that plate be sitting there when I come back. I know I will not be able to resist it." Jim bravely looked away and began his journey around the block. When he returned, both to his relief and disappointment, the plate in the window had vanished.

"Maybe they have some dog scraps they would give me," thought Jim. Walking to the back of the restaurant, he found the owner. "Sir, would you have some dog scraps that you could spare?" he asked. "My dog is really hungry,"

The kind man quickly surveyed the lean boy with starving eyes in front of him. "You know, I think I do have some dog scraps tonight," he began. "Does your dog like potatoes and gravy, with meatloaf and green beans?" inquired the man with a little twinkle in his eye.

"Does he ever," Jim quickly responded, his mouth watering in anticipation.

"Does your dog like bread and butter? And does he like apple pie?" continued the man as he carefully studied the starving boy before him.

"Oh yes, sir, he loves that," Jim said with growing enthusiasm.

"And does he have two legs, weigh about 115 pounds, wear pants, and maybe hasn't eaten all day?" smiled the man with the sparkle still in his eye.

"Sir, you got it all right except the part about one day. It's been three days since my dog has eaten!" Jim's face broke out in a smile as he realized that God had touched this man's heart with a spirit of generosity.

"Thank you, Father, for hearing my cry once again," Jim prayed silently as he walked over to the table. He was about to enjoy a meal that could have been Thanksgiving.

This kind restaurant owner demonstrated the Good Samaritan spirit on several subsequent visits by a very hungry young boy. Jim has been forever grateful to this man who demonstrated kindness and love rather than the neglect and abuse that had characterized nearly every day of his life.

Once again Jim received a tip that the detective was on his trail. "Perhaps Rapid City, South Dakota, would be a safe haven," he thought. With only enough money for a few gallons of gas, Jim watched his last few pennies flow into his gas tank. He felt lonelier than ever as he drove away from another town that he had hoped would allow him to discover happiness. Jim learned to talk more and more with the God he could not see. As he drove along, he listened to His still small voice comforting and reassuring him. His Father in heaven had not forgotten him.

It was now winter in the Dakotas with chill factors dropping to -90 degrees, making it dangerously cold for anyone exposed to the outdoors for any length of time. Jim could not keep from looking at the gas gauge that continued to predict a stop along the road, miles before reaching Rapid City. Without much warning, his car sputtered and came coasting to a stop along the highway. "Lord, please help me keep from freezing to death way out here," Jim prayed.

Within a few minutes the temperature inside the car felt the same as outside. If he did not get some help soon, he would not live long. The prospect of freezing to death inspired Jim to attempt hitchhiking to Rapid City. Fortunately, a compassionate traveler spotted a very cold boy along the side of the road and drove him into town.

"Where are you going young man?" inquired the driver.

"I don't really know, sir. I thought I might find work in Rapid City."

"Well, in that case I will drop you at the bus station until you make up your mind. At least you will have a warm place to wait," offered the driver.

Jim had only partially begun to thaw his frozen body when he found himself being dropped off in front of the bus station. Thanking the man for the ride, he walked across the street. He was thankful he at least had a place to escape the bitter cold. As he opened the station door, a cold blast of air accompanied him. The row of padded chairs near the back of the station looked like just the spot to warm up and try to decide what to do next.

The ticket agent eyed this young, haggard-looking boy with suspicion as he called from behind the counter, "Where do you think you are going young man?"

"I was hoping to warm up for a few minutes. I just got into town and have nowhere to go," Jim admitted with a very pleading look on his half-frozen face.

"We don't allow vagrants in our station. You will have to find some other place to sit," scolded the agent.

"But sir, I have no other place to go. Couldn't I just warm up for a few minutes?" pleaded Jim.

"You heard me the first time, boy. If you don't want me to call the police, you better disappear as fast as you came in," sneered the agent.

Jim slowly walked to the door to face the bitter cold once again. Out on the street he could not help but envy the warm winter clothes that protected shoppers as they ran from their cars to the stores. His thin clothes just would not keep out the cold. Walking aimlessly, he knew he would not last much longer as his body began to react with a pronounced shivering attack.

"Lord, I wouldn't mind dying. At least there would be no one to treat me mean. I wouldn't always be starving, freezing, and homeless. If I am going to live, You will have to take care of me," prayed Jim as he shuffled along the sidewalk.

Down the street the neon light displaying the sign POLICE above the door seemed to be his only remaining option. As Jim walked through the door he was relieved to see the warm friendly face of a kind police sergeant standing behind the desk.

"You look like a rather frozen young man," greeted the sergeant.

Looking pleadingly at the officer Jim said, "Sir, I really need a place to sleep for the night. Is there any way that I could sleep in here?"

"I can't let you sleep in front, but for a dollar I will give you your own cell," replied the kind officer. Reaching in his pocket he handed him his last dollar.

With a twinkle in his eye the officer replied, "I will have to call you by six tomorrow morning because our detective comes in at seven, and he loves to ask questions. I am sure you won't have time for that now, will you?"

Jim breathed a sigh of relief as he followed the officer to a jail cell. Jim had never thought being locked in jail would feel so good. "Thanks so much sir. I really don't know what I would have done without your help tonight," Jim said, looking into the kind eyes of the officer.

Just as the officer had promised, he woke Jim promptly at six to avoid the questions of one of the city detectives. Jim remembered hearing that the air force base needed men to construct additional hangers.

"If I could just find a warm place to wait for a couple of hours and a little food, I think I will be all right," Jim thought as he tried to formulate a plan for survival. He looked heavenward once again, talking to the only Father he had ever had. "Father I am trusting You once again to help me find my way. I am cold and hungry, and I don't know where to turn. Please help me."

Rewarding his simple faith, God had often spoken back to His lost and lonely child trying to find his way in a cold and cruel world. Shuffled along the sidewalk with the sun trying to thaw its way through the icy clouds, Jim noticed a café. Crossing the street and entering the café, Jim took a seat at the counter. The warm air felt good, but his stomach loudly reminded him that it had been a long time since food had paid a visit. Jim wondered if God had any kind people in this town who would help him as He had in the past.

The smile from the man behind the counter gave Jim enough courage to ask for a piece of toast and a cup of coffee.

"You look hungrier than a slice of toast, if I am not mistaken. I think you could eat a heaping plate of food," replied the owner of the café.

"I sure could, sir, but I haven't any money until I get paid from my job at the air force base," Jim said studying the eyes of the large man in the white apron.

"You just have a seat over there young man. I have a special this morning just for new employees at the air force base," informed the restaurant owner.

In a few moments Jim's breakfast came piled high on a plate. He didn't need to be reminded to say a little thank You to his Father in heaven. He had impressed the heart of another person to extend an act of kindness.

The smiling man in the white apron came walking over to his table just as he finished the last bite of his breakfast banquet. Placing a large brown bag on the table, he said in words that seemed to be coming from heaven itself, "Here is your lunch. When you get back to town tonight come back for supper. Then I will have a room waiting for you at my hotel across the street. You can pay for your room by watching the front desk on the weekends."

Jim felt one of the biggest smiles that he could ever remember break across his face as pondered the gift of kindness that God had blessed him with. It was one excited young man who reported to work that morning. For the next several months he worked at the air force base during the week and the motel on the weekends. Little by little the café owner nourished a starving young boy back to health. By the time the job ended at the air force base Jim felt like a new man. Truly God had shown Himself faithful.

In search of work, Jim moved next to Boulder, Colorado. A rancher in need of help provided Jim with his next job and a place to stay. Jim worked diligently for long hours each day. He was so thankful to find a family that really did take care of him. All his needs were met, but his heart longed to know and understand something he had only observed from a distance.

Jim felt lonelier than ever as he looked heavenward once again. "Father, I have tried to be a good boy. I have tried not to break the law or get into any trouble. I know You have taken care of me this far, but I am so lonely I am not sure I want to live anymore. Maybe I should just end it all. Lord, if You could help me once more, I sure would like to meet someone to love, someone to share my life with. Thank You for always being there for me throughout my life. I know I can trust You with this need too."

Not long after, Jim met a young lady named Phyllis Shaver. Jim instantly knew that God had sent Phyllis to fill his empty heart with love. As Phyllis wrapped her arms around Jim and embraced him with a kiss, Jim thought his heart would melt on the spot.

After spending two and a half years in Phyllis's school of love, Jim was positive marriage was his only option. Phyllis was a Christian and encouraged Jim to continue his friendship with the One who had repeatedly cared for him and arranged their union. Together they formed a Christian family and home.

Jim's life continued to progress from one providential experience to another. It would not be possible to include all the miracles that continue to surround Jim's life. I will conclude this abbreviation of his story with one last experience.

Jim joined the air force and soon became an accomplished pilot and part of a multi-force unit flying missions in Asia. Over and over God miraculously spared Jim's life. Jim looked heavenward with thankfulness to the God who had spared him every step of the way.

Jim returned to the United States for a period of service after completing his assignment in Asia. One day he was instructed to make a flight from Florida to Cannon Air Force Base in Clovis, New Mexico. It was a beautiful day to be in the sky filled with cumulous clouds and dazzling sunlight. Jim was in the pilot's seat at the controls with his colonel seated behind him. Crossing the

Mississippi River, Jim called the control tower in Biloxi, Mississippi to verify his status as they continued their flight.

"This is two niner niner calling Biloxi tower. How do you read me?" Jim called into the radio microphone.

"Maintain present speed and altitude," responded the control tower.

Jim and the colonel flew along for a moment or two, enjoying the magical splendor of the sunlight penetrating the clouds. The silence was interrupted as the voice of another pilot flying a super sonic B58 bomber calling the control tower came over the radio. "This is 52 niner niner calling Biloxi tower."

Jim listened as the pilot proceeded to give nearly the exact coordinates he had just given, only coming from the opposite direction and traveling at 1500 knots per hour. Jim turned to the colonel with a concerned look on his face. "Hey chief, what do you think we should do?"

"You are in the driver's seat. I'll leave it up to you," came the reply.

"Lord, what shall I do? Please guide me," Jim silently prayed.

In a flash Jim heard the command from the voice that he had come to know. "Take it up 500 feet now. Don't wait! You need to get up 500 feet immediately."

Jim quickly responded by pulling back on the trim control, causing the plane to climb steadily. Just as the altimeter indicated an altitude gain of 500 feet, Jim and the colonel saw the streak of the speeding bomber fly directly under their left wing with the shriek of the jet engines trailing behind them.

At nearly the same instant the radio tower blurted out the command with a frantic state of urgency, "In flight collision, do something! Kick right! Get up! Do it now! Let's go! Do something now!"

Jim and the officer sat in shock for a moment, processing what had just taken place. Then Jim returned the message to the tower, "I am already up 500 feet."

The voice from the control tower came back once again, "Who gave you clearance to change elevation by 500 feet?"

"God did," Jim replied into the radio.

The tower remained silent as the controller now had an opportunity to contemplate all that had just transpired.

Jim's hand, still trembling from fright and shock, tightly gripped the controls, causing the plane to bounce along in the sky. All at once the clouds became ablaze with sunlight. Just in front of them the clouds appeared to be lined with a fiery, brilliant lining. Like a centerpiece in this blaze of glory appeared the outline of the face of Jesus in amazing clarity, looking directly into the eyes of Jim and the officer behind him. Then Jim heard the same gentle voice he had heard since he was a boy ask him, "Are you OK, Jim?"

Jim's eyes were misty as he stared into the face of the One who had loved and cared for him from childhood. The mist turned to tears as Jim thanked God for another opportunity to continue his life.

This experience is only one of the many times that God spared Jim's life as a pilot. If you were to sit down with Jim he could add story after story to this brief sketch of his life. One thing is for sure, if you ask Jim if God knew his name, he would not let you wonder for long.

If the Creator of the vast universe filled with planets and stars heard the faint cry of a little orphan boy, don't you think He knows your name as well?

LESA

—=•((①))•=—

The marijuana smoke curled slowly upward, twisting and spiraling. Mystical patterns danced their way to the ceiling in the dim light. With the television as her companion, Lesa sat alone on the couch getting high. Her husband, Tom, was working late. Sasha, her eleven-month-old baby, was sleeping quietly in the next room.

This scenario had been repeated so many times that it had become more of a routine than an occasional escape from reality. How different her life had become since her childhood days of walking and talking with God on the farm. After completing high school and moving from home, she had been enticed with the world of fun and excitement. Step by step, she had gone down a path leading to a meaningless existence of high to high.

Just a few years out of high school, life seemed to be going nowhere for Lesa and one of her close friends. Special relationships had come and gone. The more Lesa and Anne talked about it, the less they could see any reason to stay in their home town of Stoughton, Wisconsin any longer. One night as Lesa and Anne talked over their dreams, they both agreed that if they were going to make a change this would be the best time. With a sparkle in her eye and the magic of adventure in her voice, Lesa put their dream into motion with a challenge, "Hey Anne, let's move to Florida where the snow never flies and the sun always shines. Wouldn't it be cool to live where there is no winter? We could have year-round suntans. We need to move out of town and see a little new scenery. I can't think of a better place to do it than the state known for fun in the sun!"

With a few hasty preparations and a host of good byes, Lesa and Anne were off on their southerly journey from Wisconsin to Florida. With every crook and cranny crammed full, Anne's little Chevy left town riding low to the ground.

Fort Lauderdale was decided upon as the destination for their adventure in the sun. Both Lesa and Anne found jobs and an apartment to share. They were outgoing and friendly, so it did not take long to find a host of other young fun seekers in a city on the beach known for its parties. There was a constant flow of young tourists seeking to make the most of a vacation. The local surfers were always ready for a little fun. A limitless opportunity to party existed for those looking for excitement. Life for Lesa and Anne became work by day and party by night.

One day as Lesa entered a department store she encountered one of the department managers. Tom was a tall dark surfer from Florida. He knew how to look into the eyes of a young Norwegian in search of adventure. When it came to having fun, Tom always knew where to find it. Their friendship grew as they spent more and more time enjoying life in the fast lane together. Constant as-sociation with those using drugs quickly removed the fears that had protected her earlier. It didn't take the two young ladies from the north long to get with the program. For this group of young partiers, having a good time always began by getting high.

For Tom, using drugs had never seemed that attractive. He had been surrounded by those using drugs for much of his life. His father's addiction was a source of constant contention for the entire family. It was impossible for them to live in any one place for an extended period of time. Just as Tom and his brothers and sisters would begin to make friends and start to settle down, it was time to move again. Whenever the bills and rent accumulated to a mountain that could no longer be hidden, the family would simply pack up and move to a new location. The scenario would then begin all over again.

Pain and sadness had so dominated Tom's family that it was simply a way of life. It was all they had ever known. Fighting and arguing between his mother and father made their home a place to flee from rather than a place to come back to. They had nowhere to go for rest and protection from the hostile world around them. The pain and sadness in Tom's life escalated to unbelievable proportions as he walked into a heated disagreement between his mother and father. His dad had been drinking excessively for much of the day. He yelled wildly and ran about the house waving a handgun. It went off, with a bullet striking a fatal blow to Tom's mother, right before his eyes. Tom watched in horror as his mother slumped to the floor in a pool of blood. Numbing incomprehensible pain had just become a way to survive for Tom and his family. The drugs and alcohol he hated so fiercely at home became the same means that he used to medicate his haunting past.

After a year of fun in Florida, the call of the wild began to grow faint for Lesa and Anne. Thoughts of family, home, and friends grew stronger and stronger. The plan for a move homeward began to sound better and better. Lesa knew that a move back to Wisconsin would require some serious evaluating of her relationship with Tom. As they talked over her plan to return home, it was decided that Lesa and Anne would make the move home and Tom would come for a visit soon afterward. This plan would provide a little space and time for Lesa to think through her plans for the future and her relationship with Tom.

Soon after arriving back in Wisconsin, Tom arrived as planned. Within a few months, Lesa and Tom decided to make their relationship permanent by getting married. They rented an apartment, and life began for the Roberts family. A beautiful baby daughter named Sasha was the first to join the family. Sasha added a new dimension of happiness that blessed the lives of her two young parents. Lesa and Tom continued their life of partying with rarely a thought for God. Even though Lesa was married and had a beautiful baby daughter, she could feel something was definitely missing from her life. There just had to be more to it than this. Happiness had somehow eluded her grasp even though she had pursued it relentlessly. It was always just out of reach.

One day as Lesa looked into the eyes of her sweet little baby resting in her crib, a thought spoke boldly to her consciousness. "Is the life you are now living, the life you would want your little girl to have when she grows up?" The searching question echoed and re-echoed without relief in the recesses of her troubled soul. Lesa knew she could never offer her daughter a life filled with peace, happiness, and security if she felt such an incredible void in each of these areas herself. As she wrestled with the answer to the soul-searching question, a second thought followed. "If my lifestyle now is not good enough for my little girl to grow up in, then it really is not good enough for me either."

The haunting realities of these new convictions renewed her search for true happiness, peace, and meaning in her life. With a troubled heart she began to inquire of her friends the answer to the questions that plagued her soul without any satisfactory answers. She discovered that each of her friends was equally bankrupt in the areas of meaning and fulfillment in their lives. It was impossible for them to help her find something they had not discovered. Day after day her search continued.

One day in the midst of her struggle, a thought came to her troubled mind. Perhaps God was really the missing ingredient. As she pondered this new thought, a counterattack came rushing in. "You have already tried God. He didn't supply your need then, so why would you want to try Him again?"

As a young girl Lesa had always felt close to God. Growing up on a farm provided opportunities for many a walk in the fields of tall grass decorated with wild flower arrangements of all colors and sizes. The sweet perfume of the wild flowers, with a backdrop of fleecy white clouds, birds, and butterflies, had inspired many a walk. The God she talked to by her bedroom window night by night continued to bless her as she walked and talked to Him in the fields. As she was growing up, everyone in Lesa's family knew that she and God had a special friendship.

Lesa discovered that her family's knowledge of her friendship with God could be used to her advantage. Using a few tactical strategies from her self-taught childhood psychology she advanced her cause. In winter, very little heat from the downstairs made it up the stairway to the bedrooms above. Thick frosty ice not only collected on the outside of the windowpanes, but grew thicker and thicker on the inside of the windows as the Wisconsin winters became progressively colder. One wasted no time changing into pajamas in this igloo-bedroom. A mad dash for the warmth that could be generated beneath the thick pile of blankets followed.

The last one to finish the split second pajama-changing maneuver was expected to turn off the light before making the plunge into bed. In the frantic pace of rushing for relief from the arctic temperatures, there were times when the light remained fully illuminated with both Lesa and her sister Kristi under the covers. Both insisted they had slipped beneath the covers before the other.

"I was in bed first, so you have to turn the light out," Lesa would begin.

"Oh, no you weren't! I jumped into bed while you were blinking your eyes. You just thought you saw me standing by the bed," Kristi countered. Though a little younger, she was not to be taken at the I-was-in-bed-first game.

Back and forth the I-was-first claims went until it became clear that an "I give up, you win. I'll turn off the light," would not be forthcoming any time soon from either. After waiting for a strategic period of silence, Lesa would use her ten-year-old psychological tactics. Kristi's knowledge of her love for God was her final play. From somewhere under the covers, Kristi could hear Lesa's voice, "God will love the one best who turns out the light."

It wasn't that Kristi didn't know or understand the psychological maneuver her sister was using. She understood the entire process clearly, but what if, just what if, Lesa was right and God would think she didn't love Him because she stayed in bed. Not wanting God to think she loved Him less, she would begrudgingly slip from beneath the covers. Racing for the light switch and back to the covers ended the contest.

From time to time Kristi would offer pertinent comments, providing clarification of her position. Lesa would then smile from beneath the covers. Her tactics had saved her from another encounter with Antarctica. She could take a comment or two; she was the one warm and under the covers. Looking back on her tactics Lesa has concluded; the possibility exists that it really was not the inspiration of God that directed her plan.

There could be little doubt that Lesa had experienced a very real and personal friendship with God as a little girl; now, clouds of doubt overshadowed every meaningful memory from her childhood. Her search for happiness felt like it would elude her forever.

The movie on television began to captivate her attention as the marijuana smoke thickened in the room around her. A man and his wife chasing flying saucers had contacted a spaceship and been taken aboard. They questioned the aliens about the universe, the position of earth, and the place they had traveled from.

Sitting in the midst of a smoke-filled room, high, and yet thoughtful at the same time, a thought suddenly penetrated her consciousness. "I wonder if those beings know where heaven is."

Like a bolt of lightning with impacting force, a voice full of power and authority spoke to Lesa's inner soul, "If Jesus came to-night, you would not be saved!" This voice totally neutralized the effect of the marijuana that had been so prevalent only a moment earlier. Her mind was clear. Until this impacting moment of truth jolted her consciousness, Lesa had supposed that she was probably OK. Now she knew she must re-evaluate the condition of her soul. Always before, the thought that she was not as bad as criminals and other blatant sinners had been able to quiet her conscience. Now all the "I'm not that bad; I'm OK" feelings were gone. It was a sobering thought: if Jesus should return at that moment she would be lost! The true condition of her soul rose before her. The overwhelming sense of condemnation dictated that something had to change. How to accomplish the change remained a mystery.

All night and through the next day the haunting words, "You are not saved," echoed in her mind. As the day of conflicting emotions came to an end, the urge to find escape from a guilt-ridden conscience compelled her to relieve the stress by getting high. This had become her method of problem solving. Once again, Tom was working and Sasha was sleeping. Sitting alone in front of the television, Lesa sat smoking pot, attempting to find peace. A storm was raging in her soul. The television illuminated the patterns of smoke making their way slowly toward the ceiling as before. Without warning the voice came back again, not as bold as before, but just as direct and penetrating. The somber warning was repeated, "If Jesus should return tonight, you would not be saved."

As deep conviction returned, enlightening her soul, a startling response came almost instantly into her troubled mind. The enemy of souls was not about to let go easily. He sent his own forcible impressions to her mind. He desired to continue leading her further and further away. As if the thought were her own, she heard herself respond, "I don't even believe there is a God."

This bold new declaration was a radical thought that Lesa had never seriously entertained prior to this moment. Supposing the thought to be her own, she concluded the only logical option remaining was to act upon her new statement of faith.

So began the most empty and lonely days of her life. Each time her mind replayed the word atheist, feelings of sadness would envelope her soul. This was the banner she had chosen to identify herself under. The idea that there really never had been a God attacked every fond memory of her childhood. Her warmest memories were centered on a God who had been close and personal. He had filled her life with gifts of peace and happiness. Time after time she had felt this special closeness. The more she tried to convince herself of her new ideology, the more lonely and hollow she felt. Each day felt as though she were attending the funeral of her closest Friend. However hard she tried to uphold her new position as an advocate for a universe without God, she remained a weak supporter at best.

At the end of four long miserable weeks, the first of a series of Bible study guides arrived in the mail from an organization known as The Voice of Prophecy. "This looks interesting," Lesa thought, as she examined the first lesson. "How did these people get my address, and how did they know to send this at the very moment I am desperately seeking answers for my life?"

Finding a Bible, Lesa carefully looked up each of the Scripture passages outlined in the introductory lesson. As she opened God's Word, a divine light illuminated her darkened soul. Verse after verse portrayed a God who loved and cared for His children on earth in a personal way. The power of the cross and the wonderful plan of salvation illuminated the Bible from cover to cover. God's Word took aim directly at the places in her heart that the enemy had been holding hostage. Like a thirsty desert traveler drinking long and deep at a long-lost oasis, Lesa drank in each new concept of Scripture. Eagerly she waited each week for a new lesson to arrive in the mail. As she concluded the series of Bible study guides, she felt as though a large collection of puzzle pieces had been wonderfully arranged into a beautiful new picture of God. The love affair of her childhood revived once again. The thrill and the addictive power of drugs and alcohol vanished; they were just gone, never to return as a temptation to her again. The words of this beautiful little gospel song became a living reality in Lesa's life:

> Turn you eyes upon Jesus
> Look full in His wonderful face,
> And the things of earth will grow strangely dim
> In the light of His glory and grace.

Like the psalmist, Lesa could say, "All my springs of joy are in You." The power in God's Word that defeated the tempter of Jesus in the wilderness two thousand years earlier, also totally defeated the author of atheism.

Much of Lesa's journey from her conversion and onward has been detailed in the story of our combined journey in our book *I Will Save You to Make You a Blessing*. The power of God's living

Word impacted Lesa's life in such a life-changing way that sharing its blessings remains her passion to this day. Lesa's ministries include sharing in churches, prisons, schools, women's retreats, study groups, and Christian radio. The most profound advocate of atheism today would find it a rather daunting task to convince her there really is not a personal Savior and Creator God.

If the Creator of the vast universe filled with planets and stars would seek out one of His lost children at her most defiant and rebellious moment, even denying His existence, don't you think He knows your name as well?

JASMINE

—⊶«(●)»⊷—

As a little girl growing up in a farmhouse in Wisconsin, Lesa learned to pray. Each evening before bed, she would kneel on her prayer pillow, beneath her upstairs bedroom window, to talk to God. Year by year her friendship grew. Never did she kneel on her pillow and come away disappointed. Each encounter was rewarded with the warmth of His presence.

As she grew older, becoming a wife and a mother, she realized her need to keep her special appointment with God. A special prayer pillow under her bedroom window became her secret place with God once again. Kneeling on her pillow, she invited God to take her life in His hands to mold and shape as He pleased. Her prayer window became the place she talked to God about challenges, disappointments, and discouragements. She loved to offer up praises and thanksgivings in song. Often, special people would come to mind who needed God's intervention. These also were lifted up in prayer. The prayer window became her place of power and strength throughout her years as a mother of several children with constantly changing needs.

As a grandmother, the prayer window became an increasingly important place to bring her adult children before the throne of grace. With each passing year the needs of those she loved seemed to become more urgent. Many a spiritual battle was fought before this special window.

When Jasmine was three, she and her mother Jacqlyn returned to our home to regroup and refocus. Jasmine loved to sit and listen to the stories from *My Bible Friends* written for small children. She loved to sing songs into her microphone, which could be anything within reach. She loved to perform special music for worship. She also learned to talk to God in prayer with simple but beautiful conversations that inspired all close enough to hear.

One morning Jasmine went in search of Grandma. Finding the bedroom door partly ajar, she peered through the crack at her grandma kneeling before her prayer window. She instantly became intrigued with what Grandma was doing in front of the window. With a little rustling of her feet and the sound of the door slowly swinging open, she announced her entrance.

"What are you doing, Grandma?" questioned the little voice standing in the doorway.

"Come here, and Grandma will show you," Lesa invited.

As Jasmine stepped over to the window, equipped with a prayer pillow, she began inquiring about the many articles resting on the windowsill. "What are those folded hands for, Grandma?" she began.

The carving of two hands clasped in prayer with the inscription "Prayer changes things" had become part of the permanent furnishings of the windowsill. "Jasmine, these hands remind us that when we pray to God, He can do special things for people we love," Lesa answered.

Jasmine's eyes looked for a moment or two at the praying hands and then back to her grandma, attempting to understand more of this sacred place. "What is this little black lamb for?" Jasmine wondered as she looked at a small stuffed lamb on the windowsill.

"The little black lamb reminds me of people who loved Jesus once but have wandered away and gotten lost. We can be thankful Jesus knows how to find them and bring them home," explained Grandma.

Once again Jasmine's eyes looked intently at the little black lamb, trying to understand all that it might represent. "What's in that little box, Grandma?" came the next inquiry.

"This box has all the names of special people I pray for every day. Let's look inside for your name. Look, Jasmine. Here is your name. See? It is on the same color of paper that your mother's is," Lesa said, looking into Jasmine's beaming eyes.

Excited to know that her name had been included in Grandma's special prayer box, she listened intently as the names of aunts, uncles, cousins, and other family members were drawn from the box, each identified by separate colors of paper. She seemed intrigued with the concept of removing the names one by one, each day bringing them to Jesus. "What is this pretty flower in the window for, Grandma?" continued her inquisitive little mind.

"I picked those as a gift for Jesus. Even though He made all the flowers in the world, I thought He might like a gift from me. He gives me so much, I just thought it would be fun to bring something for Him," Lesa concluded. She considered it a special privilege to pass on some of her favorite secrets of talking with God.

From that day on, Jasmine joined Grandma at the prayer window whenever she had the opportunity. She loved to talk to Jesus. Even though she was only three and could not read, she quickly memorized the colors that matched each name in the little prayer box in the window. Name by name, she would join in as she and Grandma prayed for each person in their family. Listening to Jasmine intercede was an inspiration in itself. Many days it was Jasmine's prayers that lifted the spirits of her grandma. Little Jasmine had discovered that "In God's presence is the fullness of joy."

One day it was Grandma's turn to be the observer. Early one morning she heard a shuffle beside her bed. Sitting up quietly she discovered the cause. There was Jasmine, kneeling on the prayer pillow before the window. One by one she took the names from the little box resting on the windowsill. Very tenderly, she held up each name to Jesus, asking Him to bless them in a special way. This time it was Grandma who was waiting in awe of communion she dared not interrupt. Even though she was only three, Jasmine and Jesus had become intimate friends.

If the Creator of the vast universe filled with planets and stars has time to incline His ear to the prayers of a three-year-old girl, don't you think He knows your name as well?

ISIDRO

Everyone in the little mountain village froze in their tracks as the guerillas, brandishing machine guns, stepped out of the jungle. Little children pressed close to their mothers' sides, not making a sound. The old men stood motionless, just staring in unison with a feeling of helplessness at the small band of soldiers marching steadily toward them. The young men retreated quietly into the shadows of their simple homes, hoping not to be noticed. All they could do was wait for the dreaded visitors.

"Mamma, are those men Sandinistas?" whispered a little boy staring at the band of intruders marching into his village.

"Yes, Pedro, they are. Now be very quiet and don't say a word," cautioned his mother. The entire village could only hold their breath and wait for what they knew would follow.

The civil war in Nicaragua, between the Sandinistas and the Contras, had been raging for some time. This was a ferocious battle with communist governments funding and supporting the Sandinistas and the United States funding and supporting the Contras. Sophisticated arms and equipment supplied by superpower governments provided both armies with high tech fire power. Intelligence teams trained interrogation units in torture techniques that would encourage prisoners to provide information.

The common people were caught in the middle. It was assumed that everyone was either on one side or the other. If the Contras came to a village requesting assistance and it was denied or begrudgingly rendered, the person was assumed to be allied with the Sandinistas. If the Sandinistas came for a visit, they would make the same assumptions. It was not uncommon for young men to be shot in the streets of their hometown for not willingly joining forces with a guerrilla band invading their village. Terror reigned for all calling this part of the world home during these years of war. There simply was no place to hide.

Isidro wasted no time retreating inside his house, as did all the other young men of the village. The Sandinistas marched boldly down the street. Any minute they would surely stop to demand food and water from any family of their choosing. Isidro was in his late teens and a prime candidate for an on-the-spot draft procedure that would surely follow the soldiers' feeding frenzy. Which unfortunate home would be selected, no one knew. Isidro's parents were Christians and prayed silently for God's protection for their son. Perhaps Isidro would be overlooked, and the soldiers would march out of town without seeing him.

With full stomachs, the Sandinistas began a house-to-house search as the routine recruiting process began. "Volunteers" were always in demand to replace the casualties of this brutal war. The process was as simple as it was effective: any young man from his teens to forty was eligible. Refusing to volunteer indicated he was a sympathizer with the enemy. Enemies were eliminated.

Isidro held his breath as the soldiers walked up to his door. "Lord, I am trusting in You," he prayed silently.

A broad smile broke across the face of the soldier in Isidro's doorway as he called to his commander to join him for the drafting of a new recruit.

"What is your name, young man?" demanded the commanding officer.

"Isidro," he replied softly, trying hard to be brave.

"Isidro, you are now a Sandinista," declared the officer.

"Sir, that will be impossible! You see, I am a Christian, and I can not kill anyone," pleaded Isidro.

"Evidently, you did not understand what I just said, young man. You are a Sandinista," repeated the officer.

"Sir, as a Christian I can not be a Sandinista," insisted Isidro.

The commanding officer's face reddened as he shouted, "Young man, this is your last chance. You are now a Sandinista!"

Isidro cried out to God, "Lord, what shall I do? Please help me." Like a flash the answer came clearly into Isidro's mind. "Sir, I have learned to cook quite well from my mother, and I could serve you as a cook if that would be acceptable," Isidro calmly replied.

The commanding officer was taken by surprise by the composure and confidence demonstrated by the young man standing before him. He had never encountered a situation or a young man like this! All at once his face softened as he thought of food that could actually be enjoyed. "Isidro, you are now a cook in the Sandinista army. Collect your things and come with us," the officer said with just a hint of a smile.

As Isidro looked back at his mother and father, he felt like Joseph being taken as a slave to a far country. What would it be like to be in the army? He prayed that God would keep him faithful in whatever trial he might face. He silently talked to God as he marched along with the little company of guerrilla soldiers. At times they paused, carefully rerouting their course to avoid their own land mines.

After a long, hot walk, they came to a little clearing in the jungle with some crude shelters that would be base camp and home for the new Sandinista cook. Isidro was shown to the makeshift kitchen to begin preparing for the next meal. In a few moments a boy even younger than Isidro was ushered into the kitchen. He was obviously a very scared soldier. Isidro's homesickness was forgotten as he observed the fear and loneliness in his new helper and companion. He resolved to be a friend and encourager to his new kitchen aide.

The days were long and hot, cooking for large groups of men in crude accommodations. Often, as they ate their meals, Isidro listened to the soldiers recount and relive their day of glory in the slaughter of the enemy. Other days were filled with silence and sadness as some of the men who had eaten breakfast with them that morning had fallen in battle and would not be returning. It was a constant reminder of the horrors of war.

As he worked, Isidro continued to pray that God would help him be the best cook he could to these men who faced such a horrible existence. In time he discovered that most of the men with hard exteriors were not so hard inside. Days seemed to run together. Weeks disappeared in such rapid succession that he could hardly keep track of time. God was blessing his diligent efforts to serve these soldiers, making their lives just a little bit brighter with food prepared the very best he could.

"The Contras have discovered our position and are moving in from all sides!" screamed one of the soldiers patrolling the little jungle fortress. Instant chaos ensued. Men ran for their weapons, pulling on boots, and looking frantically in every direction for an escape route into the jungle. The horrors of war had come to their doorstep!

Isidro peered out of the little kitchen window just as some of his company made a dash for the jungle. At nearly the same instant, machine gun fire erupted on all sides. He and his young helper were terrified beyond comprehension as their friends became so riddled with bullets that they were dismembered before their eyes. Screams of dying men pierced the air from every direction. Horror-stricken, they watched through a small opening in the wall as bullets shredded soldier after soldier just a few feet before their eyes. Others all but disappeared in explosions from hand grenades.

A weak counterattack caused an intensified response with ground-shaking explosions. Just as suddenly as the attack had begun, a deathly silence hung over the camp. The gunfire ceased. From Isidro's viewpoint it looked doubtful that many had escaped. Bodies lay everywhere. The haunting silence led them to believe they might be the only survivors.

Suddenly the silence was interrupted by the sound of heavy boots landing on the metal roofing of the building nearest the jungle. Three simple buildings had been built in a row, with the last building being the kitchen-cafeteria from which Isidro had been feeding his company. Without warning, the sound of machine gun fire erupted in cadence with the boots walking on the roof. It was apparent that this soldier had been commissioned to finalize the success of their attack by systematically sweeping back and forth across the roof with machine gun bullets, in the event that someone might be left hiding inside.

For a brief moment, the shooting stopped and the deathly silence returned to the jungle. Then the heavy boots landed on the building next in line. The deafening sound of machine gun fire erupted again, repeating the process of riddling every square foot of space inside the rooms beneath the gunman. Isidro and his companion knew it would be impossible to survive such a barrage of bullets. They also knew that their building was next in line.

"We are going to die!" the young boy sobbed, running for a lone rifle that had been left leaning against the wall.

Isidro lunged after him, catching him just before he reached the rifle. "No! We will not shoot. We are going to pray!" Isidro commanded as he pulled the boy to his knees beside him. Isidro began to pour out his heart in a passionate petition to his heavenly Father.

The sound of boots landing on the roof directly above them struck panic in the hearts of the two young soldiers. The boots stood still, and the machine gun was silent.

Earnestly, Isidro pleaded for his own life and the life of his young soldier friend. The silence on the roof continued, providing Isidro further time to cry out to God. He ended his prayer by making a covenant with God. "Lord, if You will spare my life, I promise I will serve You for the rest of my life," Isidro prayed.

Isidro and his friend looked at the roof where they knew that two boots were standing. The deathly silence continued. All at once the man on the roof took a step or two, and as the sound of boots landed on the building next to them, the two kneeling young men sighed with relief. They listened to the sound of the boots on the metal roofing as each of the retreating footsteps indicated their would-be attacker was traveling further and further in the opposite direction. One more sound of loud boots contacting the metal roofing clearly announced that the soldier on the roof was returning to the ground.

The two young soldiers stared silently at the place on the roof where the soldier had stood just a moment before, as the Contras faded into the jungle. They disappeared just as quickly as they had come. A season of thanksgiving followed as they acknowledged the miracle that had just taken place. Isidro's young helper became an attentive listener as he introduced him to the One who had just intervened so wonderfully on their behalf. The reality of the miracle was unmistakable as they looked around at their fallen friends, scattered around in every direction.

The terrible war ended soon after God spared Isidro's life, allowing him to return to his home. It was a joyous reunion as he recounted the many times and ways that God had intervened in his life. One story always stood paramount: the day God spared his life from the gunman on the roof.

Isidro had not forgotten his promise to God. He earnestly prayed he would not be like so many others who turned to God in crisis but quickly forgot Him when danger passed. He prayed that God would make him a blessing to his people, just as he had promised. As he prayed for God to show him the plan for his life, he learned of the Adventist Disaster Relief Agency.

As the directors at ADRA headquarters in Nicaragua listened to Isidro's story, they knew that God had placed His hand on this bright, young man who had made a covenant to be a servant to his fellow men. It was also evident that he had been blessed with the qualities of leadership. Plans were made for Isidro to attend a special session in the USA established for those from various parts of the world training for leadership. He didn't just attend the class; he absorbed all he could. After all, he was on an assignment for God.

Upon completion of the course, Isidro returned to Nicaragua to become one of the youngest district directors ever to serve in administration for ADRA. His extensive responsibilities included coordinating a disease prevention educational program that went throughout the countryside helping people make lifestyle changes. They also taught simple nutrition classes along with agricultural practices that would improve the productivity of their farmland. A second department under his jurisdiction coordinated teams of medical professionals rendering aid and assistance in remote areas. Another department supplied food and nutritional food supplements to those suffering from malnutrition. And lastly, he served as a director-coordinator of any disaster relief that would take place in his district. It all added up to quite an impressive responsibility for such a young man. Isidro's attention to detail and his faithfulness to God became evident very quickly. Because of his faithfulness, God blessed him much the way He blessed Joseph in the Bible.

Isidro was not just an office administrator. He loved the people he served. Often, as members of his staff traveled out to remote areas to hold classes to improve health and eliminate disease, he volunteered as a presenter. One day he agreed to teach a nutrition class for young mothers. As they pulled into the little mountain village, people came from everywhere. They invited the villagers to be seated as the class began. Soon it was Isidro's turn to explain the need to feed babies and small children a diet that would keep them healthy. He also used charts and scales that helped mothers see the appropriate height and weight for their children. After answering a few questions, he stepped back to casually interact with the villagers as other presentations were being made.

As the class continued, he began to get acquainted with the man standing next to him. After a few minutes of small talk, the subject of the recent war surfaced. Each had experienced more than they cared to remember. They exchanged several stories. Isidro learned that the man talking with him had been a Contra. His new friend listened intently as he began to share the story of the horrific attack on their jungle fortress, describing each detail that made up the most unforgettable day of his life. He shared the horror that he and his young helper had felt as they heard the boots and machine gun fire moving steadily in their direction. He ended his story by telling the listening villager of his prayer and the miraculous deliverance that God had worked on his behalf.

The man stood quietly listening to every detail of the experience that Isidro was reliving. As he finished his story, there was a long moment of silence. Finally the man spoke. Looking directly at Isidro he said, "I was the man on the roof that day. I was the one holding the machine gun ready to purge the building you were in. Just as I was about to pull the trigger, I heard you praying, and I could not shoot. I tried to pull the trigger, but I could not. I soon realized that something out of the ordinary was happening, and it had to do with your prayer. I felt the need to get away from your building and return to my companions." Isidro and the man stood, just staring at each other, as they realized it was more than an unlikely coincidence that they were standing side by side at this moment.

Isidro knew that God had arranged this meeting that would forever testify of His personal love for him and His power to answer prayer. If you were to meet Isidro and ask him if God knows his name, there would be no doubt in his mind.

If the Creator of the vast universe filled with planets and stars knows the name of a young man high in the mountains of Nicaragua, don't you suppose He knows your name as well?

A POOR PEASANT WOMAN

———◈———

Perhaps you have had times when you have felt like God knows the names of the important people on planet earth, and you are quite certain your name is not on His list. The enemy of God, the father of lies, loves to portray a distorted picture of God. If he can convince you to believe your status with God is in question, he knows you will soon stop praying. If he can convince you that God isn't listening, you will probably conclude—what's the use? Over and over again God has demonstrated to the human family that He is not a respecter of persons; He passionately loves each of us as if we were His only child. A brief encounter with a poor peasant woman is a beautiful picture of just such a God.

It was time for the annual board meeting at the little mission school in the Dominican Republic. I agreed to return for a few days to offer encouragement and suggestions with other board members. After experiencing first hand the need and poverty of the people in this remote little spot, I always looked for items to include in my suitcase that I knew would be appreciated by those living so sacrificially. Just when I thought I had finished the task, I happened to look up on the shelf above a spare closet. Two folded blankets lay on one side. I tried to figure out how I could possibly squeeze two more bulky items into my suitcase. As I was weighing the need for blankets on a tropical island, I remembered many a night in the winter months when a cool breeze made covering up a prerequisite to sleep. I felt impressed to bring them along even though it meant sitting on my suitcase to close it. With bulging suitcase, I made my way to the airport and onto the plane.

The road from the airport to the mission was the same bumpy, two-hour trip as always. When I arrived, it was good to see the progress that had been made to the buildings and grounds since my last visit. Truly, God was blessing this little mission, making it a light in the midst of poverty and superstition. A new face came out to meet me as I climbed out of the truck.

"Hello, my name is Stella," came from one of the brightest, smiling faces I had ever seen. So this was Stella, the nurse, teacher, spiritual leader, gourmet cook, and mother of all who called this little mission home. She had a way of instantly making a person feel welcome.

Stella had been invited to join the staff of the mission as a medical instructor and nurse for the people in the surrounding villages. Leaving her friends and family in Columbia, South America, she had joined the staff at the little mission. The war between Cartel guerillas and government soldiers attempting to retain power was intensifying. The health institute where she received her training was situated directly between the two forces fighting for supremacy. No one had to be told twice to remain on the floor during battles with bullets whizzing overhead first in one direction, then with an answering barrage from the other. This quiet and peaceful little mission in the Dominican Republic with waving palms, banana plants, orange and mango trees, pineapple fields, and a large garden was a welcome reprieve.

It didn't take long to see how much Stella was appreciated. People living in the surrounding region would carry their sick for long distances for her loving care. It was thrilling to hear how God had blessed, using simple, natural treatments to work medical miracles. Often, spiritual healing would be accompanied with physical healing. Through prayer and simple faith, God had healed several persons with critical conditions that doctors had turned away as incurable.

After a couple of enjoyable days of interaction, the scheduled board meeting began. It was those of us who had come to do the encouraging that received the encouragement at this meeting. Truly it was an inspiration to see the evidence of God's blessing in the many endeavors of the mission. The meeting concluded late in the afternoon with most of us scheduled to return to the airport the next day. The evening was spent socializing and sharing stories of the many ways God had blessed and protected.

The cool breeze that blew in after the sun set reminded me of the bulging blankets that still lay packed in my suitcase. After ending a conversation, I felt impressed to go and get the blankets. I wasn't sure who might need one, but I knew someone who would know: Stella. Walking back to my room, I quickly removed the blankets and began to search for Stella. After inquiring from a few people still visiting under the stars, I learned that she was in a room being used to house and treat patients. Walking up to the door with the blankets under one arm, I knocked quietly, trying not to disturb those who were no doubt resting. After a few moments, I knocked again. "Stella, are you there?" I called.

From inside one of the rooms I could hear a faint, "Come in."

I began to walk in the direction of Stella's voice. Reaching the doorway to one of the rooms, Stella and I met. "Stella, do you know anyone who would like some blankets?"

Stella stood in the doorway just staring at me holding the blankets. I instantly sensed I had interrupted something. After several moments of silence, Stella said, "Do you know what we were doing when you knocked?"

"No, what were you doing?" I asked.

"Come in here with your blankets for a minute," Stella replied.

In the candlelight I could see a poorly dressed peasant lady. Her leathery face was lined with creases from years of exposure to the hot, tropical sun. It was plain that life had been a constant challenge for this ailing old lady. Her fragile frame was little more than a skeleton. She sat on the edge of the bed, probably wearing everything she owned. Her gaze was fixed intently in my direction, though I knew she had not understood a word of our English conversation.

After a moment of my taking in the situation, Stella continued, "We were praying for blankets. This little lady is sick, and we invited her to stay even though we were out of space and bedding. She has been shivering on her cot, unable to sleep. After telling her I had no blankets left, I told her we should ask God for some blankets. He would know where we could find some."

Standing there, holding two blankets, I sensed that God had drawn near to remind each of us of His personal care and concern for our needs. As I passed the blankets over to Stella, a broad smile swept across the face the shivering lady. She knew she was one of God's children and He had heard her prayer.

I stood there, calculating the sequence of events that God had arranged. His timing was perfect! The blankets arrived at the precise moment of this ailing lady's prayer. Truly, God had heard the cry of one of His weary, worn children two weeks before she uttered the words. As she wrapped herself tightly in her new blanket, she had no doubt in her mind that God knew her name.

If the Creator of the vast universe filled with planets and stars can hear the faint cry and see the shiver of a poor peasant woman, don't you think He knows your name as well?

RICH

⟫⟨⟪

As the last heavy steel door closed behind us with a thud and the mechanical lock securely engaged, we were reminded once again that this was indeed a maximum-security prison. We walked just a few paces down the corridor and into a small holding area separating the prison entrance from the prison yard. Our eyes followed the long double rows of high fencing equipped with motion detectors and topped with coils of razor wire stretching far into the distance in either direction. The high towers positioned strategically around the prison yard manned with armed guards further confirmed we were not taking a Sunday stroll in the park. A loud buzz followed by a click signaled the release of the electronic lock. The tall gate opened, and we began our walk toward the prison. A wide courtyard separated the prison building from the imposing fencing and the freedom just out of reach on the other side.

It was Mother's Day; a day that had proven to be a wonderful blessing to us many times in the past. Holidays for those in prison, however, declare a sobering reality. In the eyes and faces of each of those confined within its walls, it is a matter of just getting past it. For several years, Mother's Day had been assigned to our worship team. True North, an acoustic bluegrass gospel ministry, together with Lesa and myself, had enjoyed the privilege of providing the worship service for hundreds of men and women searching for meaning in their lives. At each of the previous services our lives had been thoroughly blessed and enriched as we experienced God opening heaven's windows, pouring out grace and mercy to hurting worshipers. We knew this day would also be a wonderful experience with God, not only for prisoners, but for us as well.

As we made our way up to the main prison entrance, I couldn't help smiling as I realized that God is able to create a sanctuary for worship wherever He chooses. Chaplain Rogers warmly welcomed us as we walked along the sidewalk. Our arms were laden with musical instruments and our hearts were filled with the Word of God. Prayerful petitions for all who would be joining us in worship flowed heavenward. One more double set of mechanical steel doors at the main security center and entrance to the prison building, and we began our walk down the long concrete block hallway. Looking in either direction, it appeared to stretch without end.

Reaching the multipurpose auditorium we could feel a special atmosphere of God's grace surrounding and empowering us. The auditorium would be a worship center for hundreds of broken persons feeling a desperate need. As we walked through the door to greet the chapel staff, we silently prayed, "Father, let these wounded men and women catch a glimpse of your Son's amazing love for them today through the words of each song and Scripture passage."

Rich, an assistant to the chaplaincy, was always one of the first to greet us and offer his assistance. As we entered the auditorium, Rich stood waiting for us with a warm smile and welcome. Each one of us had observed the gracious, peaceful atmosphere that surrounded him as he assisted our ministry team. We could tell he really desired to make worship for the inmates as meaningful as possible. Seeing the peace and happiness on this inmate's face boldly proclaimed to all that Jesus had changed his life. Rich had definitely experienced a spiritual heart transplant. It was impossible to miss the transformation that had so beautifully reshaped a man who apparently had not always been the man we saw before us. Seeing Rich made each of us feel like praising God once again. Right before our eyes was a living demonstration of His transforming power.

When the second worship service ended and all the prisoners had been escorted back to their cells, Lesa and I had a few minutes to listen as Rich shared some his most recent answers to prayer. As he told his story, I couldn't help feeling impressed that Rich's testimony would encourage others facing challenges and trials. Driving home, we decided to write and ask Rich if he would like to include his testimony in our book, *God Knows Your Name*. Rich gladly accepted the invitation. Sitting down with pen, paper, and a prayerful heart, he recorded his story. I believe as you read Rich's story you will agree it is another example of a personal Savior who never gives up His relentless pursuit of one of His lost sons or daughters.

Rich grew up in a home filled with the challenges of inner city life in Milwaukee, WI. His father left his mother to fend for herself; before he could remember. Home consisted of a sad, tired mom, his older brother Brian, and his sister, Kari. His mother did her best to care for her family, but raising three children alone without a profession required assistance from the state just to survive. Although Rich and his brother and sister each had a different father, they treated each other as brother and sister, just the same. Each tried to do what he could to fill the emptiness created in a fatherless home. Try as they might, they never seemed quite able to accomplish the task.

There were those times when a young boy's mind could not help wondering, "Why don't I have a dad? Didn't he love me? Didn't he want me?" Rich's young mind often returned to the unanswerable questions that troubled his heart. Constantly, he tried to understand the complexities of his life. Always he would come away without an answer. A big void in the place where belonging should have been safely tucked away continued to grow. "Maybe something's wrong with me and that's the reason my dad left me," continued the frantic reasoning of a little boy trying to understand why he had been left with just a mom to try to make his way in life.

Moving from place to place became a way of life for a family in search of meaning and an escape from loneliness and rejection. Just about the time Rich would start to become acquainted with the other kids in his new school, it was time to move again. Changing neighborhoods and schools created an insecure and shy feeling for the one who was always the new kid. Being the new kid usually meant being an outsider when it came time to play and have fun. It was a constant challenge to make friends, knowing that the next goodbye was just around the corner. Feeling like an outsider, Rich struggled through childhood, never quite sure who he was or where he was going. His mother's quest for fulfillment continued to manifest itself in moving from place to place.

The older Rich grew, the more he felt resentment and rebellion growing in his heart. He had no place to hide. The scars on his wounded heart became more and more numerous. Rich's older brother and sister had not come through the pain and heartache unscathed either. The constant disruption in their lives inspired them to seek stability apart from their mother who had spent her whole life running. She had never stopped long enough to begin the healing process in her life; now it was up to Rich to carry their boxes and bags to the truck. From now on it would be only him and his mother. Tears of resentment and loneliness fell fast and hard as he watched his brother and sister make their escape from home. Now it would feel emptier than ever. His brother and sister, the two people in his life who had shared his feelings and struggles, were vanishing out of his life.

As Rich reached his teen years, his friends became other outsiders who shared similar identities. Together they learned how to make it in a world that had dealt them a losing hand. Learning about life from other struggling young people meant learning about alcohol, drugs, and sex in the school of life. Rich and his friends were each other's teachers.

It was in the midst of this period of growing instability that Rich's mother added a new challenge to the mountain of odds rising up before him. She knew she was out of touch with her son's life, so she decided it was her turn to leave town without her son. Rich's father was contacted and informed that Rich would be coming to live with him. Perhaps his father would give him the stability he so desperately needed. Almost as soon as Rich learned of the plan for his next move, it was under way.

After fifteen years of wondering who his father was, he found himself packing up to meet the stranger of whom he had asked so many questions about while growing up: "What would he look like?" and "Why would he want me now when he hasn't for all these years?" As Rich met his dad, he discovered that he was a really cool guy who also loved to drink and smoke pot. Now he could get high with his dad at home! This new home, complete with a step-mom and half sisters, would be the stabilizing influence to help shape the direction of his life.

Rich was in high school, but had very little time to spend learning things from books. His learning continued to be in the after hours of the day. He met an old friend from one of his past schools who shared similar interests, and they began hanging out together. It didn't take long for their lives to collide head on with the law. In a short period of time they began to accumulate a long list of violations including auto theft, flight to avoid prosecution, and possession of drugs.

With the array of charges on the desk before the judge, he had no choice but to sentence the young boy before him to a rehabilitation center for juveniles. The judge was attempting to help him make an about-face before it was too late. It was in this facility that Rich was first introduced to the concept of a higher power, greater than one's self. If he would allow Him to, He would restore him to sanity.

Before this time, his only thought of God had come in a brief encounter at a Catholic school when he was very young. A little chapel on the campus drew him back repeatedly as he hoped he would encounter the Someone or something who was called God. As his mind attempted to process this greater power he was learning about, he could not help remembering his earlier quest to discover such a being. The whole concept appealed to him, but what it all meant, and how he could be helped by this mysterious being, Rich wasn't quite sure.

It wasn't long until his acquaintance with a higher power and a decision to invite His help came to a test. As his friend uncovered a smuggled bag of marijuana in front of him, his desire for pleasure quickly regained control. His desire to surrender his life to a being he wasn't sure existed was not nearly as strong as his desire to accept a bag of marijuana from a fellow student in the program. When Rich left as a graduate from his rehabilitation program, his bag of marijuana left with him. Almost as soon as he was on his own, he reunited with his old friend and partner in crime. The thrill of adventure and lack of purpose in life caused their minds to become more calculated in their endeavors. Two acts of armed robbery quickly returned both of them to correctional institutions.

Ethan Allen was a noted juvenile rehabilitation school for those needing extensive refocusing of their lives. Once again in a program for substance abuse, Rich came face to face with the reality that only a higher power could help him change his life. Contemplating his life thus far and the many choices he had made, caused him to reevaluate the direction of his life. Face to face with his undeniable need, he began to think more seriously about the Author of life and the God who could help him begin the needed untangling process. The more he attended the group sessions, the more he sensed his need. The many positive skills and activities he became involved in, such as working in the print shop, editing the school's newspaper, and playing on the football team, enabled him to finish his time at Ethan Allen on a positive note.

Rich felt he had a new lease on life as his sentence was completed at Ethan Allan. His only home was back at his father's house with all the things that had been his downfall thus far. He determined that this time would be different. He was going to make something of himself. The encouragement from the staff and his impressive test results gave him the courage to make the trip to the registrar's office of UW Milwaukee, just a short distance from home. He was going to go to college and become someone his friends and family would be proud of. With his head held high, he entered the administration building ready to begin his education. His future was just around the corner. As the registrar explained the way loans, grants, and scholarships are dispersed, and the timeline that it usually required, Rich's heart sank. His dream of receiving a degree in commercial art seemed to have been stolen in one short conversation.

Discouraged and frustrated, he stopped and bought a newspaper at a convenience store on his way home to explore the jobs section. Slumping on the couch he listlessly read through the columns of advertisements for employees. For the time being, a temporary job would apparently be his only remaining option. He answered an advertisement from a concrete construction company needing personnel immediately.

It felt good to work hard learning a new skill. The satisfaction of earning his own way made him determined to follow through with his decision to live a new life. Rich was confident that the Someone or something out there could keep him from returning to his past. He soon discovered that just knowing He was there and had the power to change him was not enough. After a short time of attempting to resist all his old friends and their destructive lifestyles, he was right back where he had left off before the state had intervened on his behalf.

The emptiness in his life created a void that could not be satisfied with relationships, things, or his constant attempts to sidestep reality with a host of self-prescribed substances. Rich attempted numerous relationships, always hoping the next would be the one that would finally meet the needs of his heart. Through one of his attempts to satisfy the deep void in his life, he became dad to a baby boy named Evan. With the best of intentions, Rich began his attempt at fatherhood. Without ever having witnessed anyone to pattern his new responsibility after, he really hadn't a clue where to begin. Looking into the eyes of his new little wonder wrapped up in his arms, he promised himself that he would never desert or abandon little Evan as he had been. Even the strong desire and dream to be a good dad to his son was not enough to hold together his relationship with Evan's mother. Rich discovered he was incapable of giving or receiving something he had never experienced. He was adrift, not knowing how or where to fill the deep void he had been seeking to fill his whole life.

When Evan was just three years old, Rich met the young lady he was sure would be the one with whom he would spend the rest of his life. She also had a boy about Evan's age who seemed to be the companion of his dreams. They were married, and soon after, a baby daughter joined the family. More than ever Rich wanted to prove he could be the father he had never had for his ready-made family. Once again he discovered the challenges of building a solid relationship. Due to his dysfunctional reference point, becoming the husband and father he desired seemed out of reach. "This time will be different," he reasoned. "I am going to do whatever it takes to make this work."

Raising a family in any city is more than a small challenge, and Milwaukee was no different. High crime areas of the city were expanding rapidly. Neighborhoods that had been relatively safe in the past became dangerous places, even in the daytime. One of Rich's close friends was held up at gunpoint just a few blocks from their home while on his way to a convenience store. A few months later a friend was shot in a car-jacking. Fear surrounded all who called these inner city areas home, but limited income made relocating impossible. It was a contest for survival one day at a time. The father of Rich's stepson became the next neighborhood victim. He was shot and killed by a young man over a dispute regarding the way he had crossed the street. Everyone in this part of town felt they were living on the edge of time, never knowing when their number would be drawn. Night by night homes in their neighborhood were broken into and burglarized as thieves took whatever they chose without much opposition. They lived in fear. What tragedy would strike the neighborhood next?

One day on the way home from work with his employer, Rich stopped at a suburban sporting goods store and purchased a handgun. "I will not allow anyone to harm my wife and kids if I can help it," he reasoned. Armed with his new handgun he felt he might have a chance for his family to survive.

Not long after his purchase, he stopped at a bar looking for a concrete contractor whom he thought might need some help. After spending only a few minutes at the bar, a man, who most probably had not just arrived, approached Rich, ranting and raving. Leaning over his shoulder and in his face, he began stating his position. With a number of derogatory phrases and an explicitness that made his point quite clear, he threatened to do whatever was necessary to protect his interest in the lady he had been acquainting himself with. It was clear to him that Rich had been trying to get the attention of the same young lady. Seeing Rich as an intruder, he finished his tirade by announcing the possibility of putting some bullet holes in Rich.

In a state of shock, Rich collected his things and walked out the door. As he neared his car in the parking lot, he spotted the man who had threatened him just moments earlier walking toward him with three of the friends who had been inside with him. The look in their eyes made it quite clear they were coming for business. Rich had seen people get jumped many times before and knew he was in trouble. Remembering his loaded gun tucked under the seat, he quickly unlocked the door and reached for it. Pointing his gun in the direction of the four men coming at him, he yelled, "Get away from me! Get away from my car! I am just trying to leave here."

In response, one of the four men coming steadily in his direction reached for a gun of his own. Ducking behind his car, Rich open fired until his gun was empty. Diving into the driver's seat, he quickly started his engine and raced out of the parking lot to the sound of return gunfire. In a state of shock and terror, Rich drove home with adrenalin surging through his body. He didn't have long to wonder what he should do next, as the ringing telephone jarred him back to reality. The frantic voice of a friend from the bar exclaimed, "One of the men at the bar was shot and killed, and the police are looking for you!"

Dropping the phone, Rich cried out, "Oh, God . . . Why?!" In a state of disbelief Rich tried to process what had just happened. He was in a real mess, and he knew it, but worst of all, someone had lost his life and his blood was on Rich's hands. His mind raced, searching for a way to solve the impossible situation he was in, but only the ominous reality of an irreparable loss hung over him like a thick cloud of darkness.

Out of this darkness a voice began to speak to him of the hopelessness of his situation. "You will never get out of this. Why don't you just end it right now? One more bullet would solve your problem forever. You are never going to see your wife and children again. So, go ahead! End it now!"

Hanging in the highly emotional and spiritual balance of life and death, Rich cried out with just one word to the One who had been called the higher power, "Why?!" If there was one thing he needed just now, it was help from a power higher than himself.

God had been waiting long for Rich to call out to Him for help. In the quietness of the long sleepless night that followed, God began to speak to one of His runaway sons. In desperation and in the darkness of this lonely night, Rich began his first real communion with his heavenly Father. The presence of God and His surrounding peace carried Rich through his surrender and arrest. Entering jail with a murder charge was a terrifying experience, but something about his conversation with God and the peace that followed, got him through the long wait for his trial.

In response to Rich's hurting heart, God began to more fully reveal Himself. Volunteers came each Sunday to share God's love in jail. Fellow inmates who had discovered a friendship with God shared encouraging thoughts and verses from Scripture. A Christian named Marge adopted Rich as a pen pal. Over and over God used her words of comfort to speak directly to Rich's heart. God was teaching Rich that He is never without the necessary resources for our healing, even if we are totally bankrupt.

Rich's dreaded day in court finally came. A lesser charge of reckless homicide resulted in a thirty-year sentence. From the courtroom it was directly to prison, a lonely, humiliating, and disorienting experience. Separation and disconnection from wife, children, and loved ones was a nightmare that could only be processed a little at a time.

Visits, phone calls, and letters from home tapered off with the "For better or for worse" feeling like it was on shaky ground. Not long after, divorce papers arrived, confirming permanent loss and separation from the one he had promised himself he would always love and protect. Every night became a nightmare, with his mind formulating vivid thoughts of some other person taking his place at home with the one he had learned to love.

During these long dark nights the enemy of souls returned to encourage Rich to end his existence. Suicide would solve it all. "The best thing you can do for your children would be to kill yourself. Don't be selfish," taunted the hellish voice.

In a state of overwhelming despair, darkness pressed in as if it would snuff out Rich's life of its own accord. Life's rope felt as though it had finally frayed its last thread, with the sensation of one long free fall into an expanse of darkness. "Maybe ending it all would be best," Rich thought.

The dark evil presence encouraged on, "You really would save everyone the burden of your existence if you would let go and end it all."

In the darkness Rich cried out a closing prayer for his life to God saying, "The fuel that kept this fire burning has run out! I see no reason to go on. . . . Forgive me. . . . Farewell!"

In the darkness of a lonely prison cell, as the tears ran dry, and an aching heart felt like it would burst at any moment, a still small voice penetrated the silence in the most soothing and comforting tone that Rich had ever experienced. With a feeling of warmth and love, Rich heard his Father speak, "My son, this is not the end for you, but only the beginning. The reasons for you to go on are far more than you can imagine."

Sitting alone in the darkness, Rich felt the father of lies quickly return with a renewed effort to press his case in a last desperate attempt to bring the life he had been leading in misery to an eternal end. From the midst of the cloud of darkness surrounding him, a commanding voice boldly declared, "Don't kid yourself. . . . Don't be one of those guys who create a psychological solution for yourself because you can't handle what you are going through! Just end it now!"

Rich could feel himself straddling a fence. Death and despair were on one side; hope for a new beginning, promised in warmth and love, on the other. Back and forth his mind went between the offer of life and the escape to death. The eternal reality of balancing on the brink of a great precipice loomed before him.

In the midst of his incredible storm of spiritual emotion, a friendly voice greeted him as another inmate came into his cell. "Hey Rich . . . I just felt impressed to stop by for a moment to let you know this is not the end for you, but really the beginning. If you will just let God have your life, He will give you so much more to live for. His plan will take you to places you could never have imagined. God really does love you. Well, I've got to go—just felt I should stop by with a word of encouragement. . . . Talk to you again later." With a smile he slipped out, leaving Rich alone once again.

"Oh God….You really are real…" Rich began to pray, "You sent someone with a message of hope just when I needed it. He just repeated the words You spoke to me a moment ago, almost word for word."

In an instant the heavy, dark cloud of oppression and the voices commanding his self-destruction were gone. For the first time in his life Rich began to feel free, even though he was occupying a cell in a maximum-security prison. The wonderful presence of God continued to grow all around him, embracing him with a security and warmth he had never experienced. Feelings of freedom reigned where feelings of doom and hopelessness had been waiting eagerly to snuff out his life. Rejoicing in an atmosphere of light and peace, Rich could now see a ray of light at the distant end of the tunnel that stretched out far into the future.

As his mind became illuminated with heavenly light, he realized that ending it all would only make things worse for his children, not better. "If I would have listened to that woeful voice, I would never have the opportunity to fulfill my promise to my children," Rich thought. "I was oh, so close to ending it all."

In the embrace of his heavenly Father, Rich basked in the realization that the One whom he had always heard about as a higher power, was really the Father he had always longed for, the Lover of his soul. In an atmosphere of "peace that passes all understanding," the Lord performed a wonderful heart transplant in Rich. Not in a beautiful sanctuary or exquisite cathedral, but in a lonely prison cell. The Master Surgeon performed the miracle of miracles. He made all things new, and Rich was born again.

Not long after Rich's life-changing encounter with God, an opening in the prison chapel became available. With his enthusiasm for God's Word and love for God written all over his face, the prison chaplaincy staff of four elected to solicit Rich's assistance in meeting the spiritual needs of his fellow prisoners. In a spirit of gratitude and praise Rich accepted his call to the ministry within the prison. It would be hard to convince Rich that his heavenly Father did not have a wonderful plan for his life. Each day he looks forward with eagerness for an opportunity to share his new-found Friend and Savior, Jesus, with others who are still lost in darkness.

Rich's story can best be concluded in his own words:

During my journey here I have completed many legs of the race: like Judas, I've betrayed; like Thomas, I've doubted; like Paul, I've perse-cuted. But like John, I've proclaimed; like Joseph, I've prospered; like Job, I've persevered. Yet like Moses, I am in the wilderness tending the sheep; my people and our Egypt is right here.

I learned that although I would love to be able to save souls by merely sharing what I know, people here react more positively see-ing a sermon than they do hearing one. I have seen many men come through here during my stay that I have known or met in my past. For example, the friend I got in trouble with back in high school has been through here twice. In addition, at least twenty others whom God has granted me the privilege of personally sharing His love with, and countless others whom I hadn't known before, are my brothers nonetheless. For now and forever I pray that God will guide me through His Holy Spirit. Pray for us, as we pray for you. Our strength is made perfect in weakness.

May God bless you all in Christ,

Rich

If the Creator of the vast universe filled with planets and stars would come to one of His wounded sons in prison at the moment his life was hanging in the balance, don't you think He knows your name as well?

LUKE

———⊂«(●)»⊃———

Our hearts were overflowing with praise as we concluded the last meeting of the prayer conference at Canadian University College near Edmonton, Alberta. Our Father, enthroned in glory, had opened the windows of heaven and showered us with His grace and mercy. A spirit of revival had been born in the atmosphere of prayer.

After a moment of giving thanks we made our way across campus to our dormitory room to prepare for our journey home. Walking along the sidewalk en route to our room, we were joined by one of the students who had faithfully attended each session of the weekend. "Hello Luke, care to join us?" I said. Luke was a large-framed French Canadian with an equally broad smile that instantly won your heart. Watching Luke as he eagerly feasted on the spiritual blessings had been like watching a sponge soak up water. He walked with us, not wanting to miss an opportunity for another blessing. Engaging in a little friendly conversation enabled us to get better acquainted. Reaching the door to my room Luke paused for a moment and said, "I would like to talk to you if you don't mind." I invited him in. As we sat facing each other on the two beds furnishing the room, Luke's face became noticeably serious and focused. "Do you mind if I tell you a little about my life?"

he asked. His sudden change in demeanor caused me to be more attentive as I encouraged him to share his story.

He began his experience in a little town in northern Alberta with a climate very closely resembling the North Pole. His family included an older brother, mother, and father. They had very few warm memories. Their parents were staying together from obligation rather than happily enjoying life together. As Luke described his home, it sounded like a mechanical routine. There was very little to strengthen relationships; faith in a loving God was a concept never mentioned or thought of. He was a total stranger in their home. Without God and without the love that comes from a close family, Luke's life lacked meaning and purpose. As he was nearing completion of high school, his father and mother divorced. His pain and loneliness grew deeper. Despair and hopelessness were constant companions. Often, he contemplated ways to end his miserable existence. Feeling empty and lonely, Luke began to search for happiness with his friends. His search for happiness included drugs and alcohol. His loneliness led him to others trying to fill the emptiness in their lives. Together they searched for a substitute for the love that was missing from their lonely hearts. After graduating from high school, partying became their main focus. After a year or two of partying, Luke felt more lost and lonely than ever. He reasoned that if this is all there is to life, then it really wasn't worth living.

One day he happened upon some booklets containing philosophies of an eastern religion. He learned about an inner peace that could be found through meditation and other religious practices. Tired of the disappointment he had experienced from drugs and alcohol, he decided to explore this new avenue for meaning in his soul. The promise of peace to be found in this new religion seemed to be beckoning him. The more he read about the eastern religions the more interested he became. Much of the material he had been reading came from Vancouver, British Columbia. He decided a move to Vancouver would be the only way to find the missing answers he was so desperately seeking. Packing a few things, he left his brother and mother and made his way to Vancouver where he soon discovered the city was home to many different gurus, cults, and temples housing religions, all of which claimed to have what his soul was searching for. Meditation that was supposed to cleanse his soul did nothing for him. The chanting mantras and smoldering incense did not fill the empty void in his soul. Rather than finding meaning and clarity for his inner loneliness, he found confusion. Comparing one philosophy with another led him on an exhausting journey. From temple to temple, guru to guru, priest to priest, he searched. His inner being was crying out for something, but for what he wasn't sure.

Luke discovered living in a big city, while being surrounded by so many people, felt even lonelier than living in a small community with familiar faces greeting you at every turn. With added confusion in his soul and the mystique of the big city gone, he decided he had to get away. Once the decision was made it took him very little time to put his plan into action. The sooner he could get going the better. His obvious dilemma was where to go. He decided to visit his mother who had moved to Quebec, at the other side of Canada.

It was nice to see his mother again. It had been some time since he had used French in everyday interactions and dialog. He enjoyed the visit but knew he could not call his mother's home his own indefinitely. Something inside continued to trouble him. After spending a few months in Quebec, Luke's restless heart prodded him on. He decided he would go back to his hometown in northern Alberta to visit his brother. As he traveled the long road back to his hometown, he reflected on all the places his search had taken him. He had to find an answer soon; his search could not go on much longer. If there were answers to be found he needed to find them, and find them soon.

Luke and his brother had always been quite close, and had learned to rely on each other in a home lacking love and abounding in pain. He could not hide his feelings any longer; he was wearing them on the outside. It was plain for all to see he was going through a very difficult time. The first weekend after his return, Luke's brother invited him to a soup and sandwich supper with some new friends he had met. He knew that a home cooked meal would touch a weak spot after many months on the road. He told him he had been joining these new friends for a special Friday evening supper followed by a Bible study for several weeks. Luke wasn't so sure he wanted to go to a Bible study but friendly faces with a good home cooked meal were just too much to pass up. Together they made their way to the Friday evening fellowship. Luke could feel the warmth and closeness that this little group enjoyed. When the meal was over they moved to the living room to sing and discuss a Bible topic. Seated next to his brother, Luke followed along the best he could. After only a few minutes of group discussion, Luke's brother leaned over and whispered, "You know that you have to go to church with these people tomorrow since you ate supper with them, don't you?" In a state of panic but trying not to be noticed by the rest of the group Luke said, "What!"

"That's right," his brother responded, "everyone who has supper here has to go to church with them."

Continuing to whisper back and forth as inconspicuously as possible Luke said, "Why didn't you say anything about this before we came?" After pondering his plight for a few minutes Luke leaned over to his brother and said, "Well, all right. I will go this once if I have to, but that's it." Much of what was said after that completely passed Luke by as he sat in the small circle, wondering how he had gotten himself into this situation. Luke learned much later that his brother had fabricated the whole story just for a little fun at his expense.

The next morning in a state of total apprehension Luke prepared for church. Convinced he had committed himself with a bowl of soup he resolved to hold up his end of the bargain. Dressed in the only clothes that he had, Luke joined his brother for the short ride to church.

Looking over at Luke seated on the bed, I observed the whole expression on his face change as he described his first visit to church. "I really didn't know what to expect as I walked up to the door, but I didn't have to wait long to find out." Luke's face was aglow as he said, "When I stepped through those doors I knew I had found what I had been searching for all those years. I could feel God's presence surround me and welcome me as I stepped into His house. Peace and joy filled my soul like I couldn't have ever imagined." Every portion of the service fed his soul—the singing, the Bible study, the sermon. From that moment Luke knew he had found a new family. His whole reason for living now revolved around his new friendship with God and the people who worshiped Him. Friday evenings found him in regular attendance for the delicious homemade bread and soup. He soon discovered an even greater hunger for the spiritual food that fed his soul following the meal. The more Luke learned the songs, the more enthusiastically he joined in as he praised his new-found Savior. The Bible became a living book. He often heard his heavenly Father speaking directly to him. For Luke, his new love affair continued to grow and grow. After several months of study and investigation in the Scriptures, Luke decided to surrender his all to the God who had so graciously led and guided him. More than once He had kept him from taking his life. There could be no doubt that a God of love knew his name! The entire congregation, Luke's new family, entered into the celebration as Luke walked into the water to be baptized. For the first time in his life he felt a wholeness in his soul. The place in his soul that had cried out with emptiness for all those years now sang with joy overflowing. Luke found the open arms of the Savior who had been patiently waiting for him. He could look back and see He had been carefully guiding the course of his life all along. The smile on his face as he came out of the water testified to the embrace of God. Luke knew he was home!

A conflict came as a result of his faith: his job. Since returning to his hometown he had been working at the video store. It was during the Christmas season that Luke made his decision to follow his Lord all the way in baptism. The streets were filled with shoppers making their final preparations for the holiday season. The twinkling lights and festive decorations lining the streets added to the romance of the season. The beauty of the season decorated stores and streets. All the trimmings were in place. As joyous and festive as they were, they were no comparison to the new-found joy and peace he had discovered in Jesus.

The usual last minute shopping rush was nearing its peak. It was just two weeks before Christmas as Luke approached his store manager with the news that he would soon be baptized. He told him briefly of his search for happiness and the recent discoveries that had filled the emptiness of his soul. He then shared his understanding of the biblical Sabbath and his desire to be faithful in keeping it. Luke informed his employer he could no longer work during these sacred hours. The store manager carefully studied the young man, scrutinizing his sincerity as he unfolded his plans to discontinue working on the video store's busiest day. When he was finished, the manager made a valiant appeal to the loyalty of his worker. Surely Luke would not let him down when his non-Christian workers faithfully served during the busiest season of the year. Luke instantly became confused. His manager reminded him Christians were to be responsible to their employers. "Luke, I am sure God will understand your responsibility and overlook your Sabbath observance until after the holidays," pleaded the manager. "Perhaps he is right," Luke reasoned. "Would God want me to let down my employer when he needs me most?" The whole concept of the Sabbath was new and at the moment very confusing. After considering the pleadings of the manager Luke replied, "I will work on the Sabbath only in case of an emergency, and you are not able to find anyone else." Surely this would satisfy the issue of loyalty and at the same time would allow him to worship with his friends. In his innocence Luke felt he had honored his Lord and remained faithful to his employer.

In northern Alberta the Christmas season lacks all semblance of tropical weather. It was -10F on the day Luke discussed the Sabbath at the video store. But this heat wave was not to last long. Luke said, "Then it started to get cold. Each succeeding day the temperature dropped nearly ten degrees." By the following Friday evening it was nearly fifty below zero. Christmas shoppers now hurried from store to store wrapped from head to toe. The cold weather only boosted video rentals as people retreated indoors. Long lines of customers waited daily buying and renting videos for the Christmas holiday. For Luke, only one thing captivated his attention: the wonderful inner joy and peace he had recently discovered in his new-found relationship with God. The cold outside could not chill his excitement and anticipation for the worship experience of the coming Sabbath. When Friday came Luke began a mental countdown of the time remaining until church would begin in the morning. Friday afternoon Luke bade his associates farewell, wishing them a happy holiday and a nice weekend. He bundled himself for the weather and began the two-mile walk home. His limited income had not been sufficient to include the purchase of a car. Walking to and from work just happened to be a fact of life he cheerfully accepted; however, fifty below zero did present a challenge. Luke spent Friday evening studying from his Bible and communing with his Father in heaven. As he laid his head on his pillow to rest for the night, the soft glow of a first love experience with God warmed his heart. His sleep had never been so sweet.

The moan of the wind outside sang an icy song to Luke as he rolled over, realizing it was Sabbath and he would be joining his brother and friends for worship. Luke shivered as he climbed out of bed. It felt as if the furnace had not done so well keeping up with the bitter cold. It was seeking entrance through any unsuspecting crack in window, wall, or door. "Brrrr," Luke said, as he made his way over to the window to peer outside at the thermometer hiding behind the layers of ice clinging to the glass. The thick ice on the inside of the window made it difficult to see the mercury level on the outside. "No wonder it feels cold," Luke thought as he spotted the mercury at fifty-five below zero. But this was Sabbath and he could ride with his brother to church rather than face the usual two-mile walk to town. After a warm breakfast Luke dressed for church and began to review his weekly Bible study lesson, anticipating the upcoming discussion at church.

Luke's concentration was interrupted by the sudden ring of the telephone. He instantly recognized the voice of his store manager on the other end of the line. "Luke, I am sorry to have to call you, but I am afraid you are going to have to come in today. It is fifty-five below zero this morning and no one's car will start. I am at the store single-handed and this is the last weekend before

Christmas. It promises to be one of the busiest days of the year. You don't drive to work so I know you can make it in. This is an emergency and you gave your word that you would come. I know you will do your Christian duty." There was a long pause as Luke contemplated going to work instead of joining those who would soon be worshiping. Finally, Luke consented to make the two-mile walk in the bitter cold in keeping with his promise a couple of weeks earlier. Fighting back tears, Luke changed from his church clothes to his work clothes. Why had he promised to go to work on the Sabbath? As he closed the door behind him it was with heavy heart that he began the frigid journey to work. Trudging along, bundled as an explorer en route for the North Pole, Luke made his way to town.

Walking into the store felt like a blast of heat after being in such extreme cold. As Luke prepared for work, his heart felt heavier and heavier as he thought about all he would be missing at church. After slipping into his work vest and adjusting his name tag, his daily work routine began. Every few minutes he glanced at his watch, anticipating what would be taking place at church at that moment. Replaying each detail of the worship service in his mind, seconds became minutes and minutes seemed like hours. Working mechanically behind the counter Luke lifted his heart in silent prayer to his heavenly Father. "Lord," he prayed, "You know how I was looking forward to singing praises to Your name. You know how I have longed to join in the worship service today. I feel so lonesome for You today, please come near and let me sense Your presence. Lord, I don't think I can make it through this day without You. Thank You for hearing my prayer. I do love You and want to serve You. Just show me the way." While customers continued their constant flow to the counter, Luke silently cried out to the Lord to help him through what felt like an eternity.

Luke looked at his watch for the hundredth time—it was only 10:00 a.m. "Lord, I have been here for only two hours with eight more to endure. I don't think I can make it." He looked up as he heard the bell on the door announce another customer entering. Each time the door opened, a cold wave of air came rushing in, reminding him of the walk home that waited for him at the end of the day. Each cold shot of air kept him very wide awake. His eye caught sight of an old man who appeared to be homeless. Perhaps he had come in just for a break from the cold. He stopped just inside the door standing in front of a large heater warming the entrance. "That's strange," Luke thought. "I know most everyone in this small town, but I don't remember ever seeing this man before." Gazing at the old man he wondered how someone could possibly survive living on the streets way up here in the north. There was something different about this old man; maybe it was the look in his eyes. Luke waited on customers, all the while watching the old man out of the corner of his eye. Each time Luke would look directly at the old man he would smile back a kind smile of encouragement. Luke couldn't ever remember seeing such kindness in anyone's face before. The more he looked and watched the old man dressed in shabby clothes, the more fascinated he became.

Luke glanced at his watch again; church should be just about to start, but he was helplessly trapped behind a counter that felt more like a prison than a store. "Lord," he cried, "I don't think I can take any more of this. I have all this time left to work and I can't take it any more." Turning toward the door his eye caught the eyes of the kind old man. He smiled back at Luke and said, "Don't worry about the time." A thrill rushed through Luke's soul as the kindness of the old man's words seemed to fill him with amazing peace from the inner storm raging in his soul. "Don't worry about the time, Luke," whispered a peaceful, soothing voice to his inner being.

Luke smiled as he felt the presence of God surround him, and closed his eyes to enjoy the moment.

He opened his eyes with a start. Glancing up at the clock on the wall, it was 6:00 p.m., the closing hour, due to the bitter cold weather and the danger it presented to travelers. He looked around the store, watching one of the last customers leave. He glanced quickly to his side at the store manager working at the register just next to him. "Have I been here all this time?" asked Luke.

"What are you talking about Luke? You know we have been so busy we haven't even been able to take a break today. This has been by far our busiest day of the year. There have been lines backed up far into the aisles most of the day. We have been working frantically all day long and you ask me if you have been here all day long. Are you feeling OK?" Luke just stared back in disbelief as he tried to imagine what might have taken place. He looked down at his bulging cash drawer. Truly this had been a record day for sales, but he could not remember even a moment past looking down at his watch just as the worship hour was about to begin. He took his cash drawer out to count and balance it. Never before had he seen so much money from one day's sales in the six months he had worked at the video store. Carefully, he counted every penny. "This is impossible," Luke thought. He counted his drawer again, only to find the same results. His drawer balanced to the penny. Never once had he arrived at a perfect balance before. Always a penny over, or two pennies under, or a nickel one way or the other, but never had he had a perfect balance before. Luke was speechless as he tried to figure out what had just taken place. He knew his boss would never understand if he tried to explain (how could he?) for he didn't understand himself. Quietly he put away his money, slipped out of his store vest and dressed for the two-mile walk home in the fifty-five below zero temperature.

Stepping into the night, he began the long walk. A short distance from the store he lifted his eyes heavenward to talk to his heavenly Father. "Father, tell me what just happened back there, I don't understand. The last thing I remember were the words of that kind old man." Luke felt the closeness of his Father surround him once again. It was with a heart overflowing with praise and gratitude that Luke looked heavenward with his prayer of thanksgiving. "Thank You for taking my place today; thank You for working my shift and providing me the blessing of rest my soul earnestly longed for." Luke realized that the God who had taken his place on Calvary long ago had come once again to take his place. Light and peace from heaven flooded his soul. His love and gratitude knew no bounds. Luke said, "As I walked home that night it was as if I was on a cloud, scarcely aware of the cold as my heart felt like it was bursting with joy and excitement from both the miracle and the incredible presence of God."

Luke sat beaming on the dormitory bed across from me as he reflected on a God who had so wonderfully cared for him all along the way. He said, "I phoned my store manager right away, informing him I would never return to work on a Sabbath again for any reason." Understanding more clearly his covenant with God, he promised the Lord that he would remain faithful by His grace for as long as he lived. Luke concluded by saying, "It didn't take me very long until I realized that a video store is really no place for a Christian to work at all. I walked away from my only job knowing that my Father in heaven was faithful. I knew He would take care of me, and here I am at a Christian university studying to be more useful and effective in any ministry that God may choose for my life." I thanked Luke for sharing his story. We bowed once again in worship and praise before a God as wonderful and kind as Luke's.

Luke walked to the door still beaming as he had just relived the whole experience with me again. "I'll see you in heaven Luke, and I will be waiting for you to tell me the rest of the story," I said, as he walked down the hall to the outer door.

I sat pondering Luke's story for a few more minutes after he left. I tried to process what God had done for one of his children trying to find his way through the darkness of planet earth. I was in awe. A pure and holy God had been willing to leave His throne in glory and go to Calvary to become sin and pay its penalty for a planet filled with the lost and dying. Our Savior so completely bore the sins of our world that it wrenched His heart in two, dying a death for you and me. This same pure and holy God had come back to planet earth to work for one of his children that he might have a Sabbath rest. Truly He said the Sabbath was made for man, and He had given of Himself that Luke might enjoy that blessed rest. I couldn't help picturing the Savior holding Luke in His arms throughout the day as he rested. What a way to spend the Sabbath, resting in the Savior's arms! Of all the places the Lord of the universe might have chosen to minister, a video store filled with every type of corruption and darkness imaginable, would certainly have been His last choice, but He came.

What wondrous love! What amazing grace! Luke's God came that you and I might have life and have it more abundantly. The only thing He asks is your special friendship in return. There can be little doubt that God knows Luke's name.

If the Creator of the vast universe filled with planets and stars heard the voice of a searching young man, don't you think He knows your name as well?

JADIS

I f you have happened by a maternity ward at just the right moment, you no doubt have witnessed the broad smiles of middle-aged individuals peering through one of the many viewing windows. A newcomer to the family has them beaming and cooing. By some, it would seem a fair assumption that these middle-aged enthusiasts smiling at a pink, wrinkly faced bundle are proud new grandparents. They may even make such a claim to other family members or a person passing by. The truth is that certain rights of passage must be encountered and successfully endured before making a rightful claim to grandparenthood.

Many memorable moments occur in this process of becoming a grandparent that begins at the hospital. At each step along the way beginning with infancy and on to toddler, scrapbook memories take place. But to earn the title of a fully certified grandparent, you must first pass the test of a sleepover by your preschool offspring, who later can be rightfully called your grandchild if you pass the test.

If you are like most of us who have been tested as grandparents, when you first heard the request, "Grandma, can I sleep at your house tonight?" it all sounded innocent enough. With warm sentiments, you eagerly anticipated this event as a special memory that would qualify for an entry in your scrapbook. You are quite certain you will want to immortalize them for eternity. For those who have not yet made such an entry, I need to prepare you for this experience that will determine the true status of your claim to grandparenthood. Perhaps you will glean useful insights that will aid in your preparation process as I relate my experience of a sleepover with Jadis, our five-and-a-half-year-old granddaughter.

The romantic scrapbook scenario was having its full affect as my wife, Lesa, prepared a cuddly, warm bed for our little sleepover guest. To qualify as a scrapbook experience, bedtime stories, songs, and prayers must precede the actual sleeping portion of the event. This can be a lengthy experience to fulfill the many requirements outlined by a creative five-year-old mind. But who said creating scrapbook memories would be easy? At the conclusion of pre-sleep exercises, it is really the grandparents who are ready to move to the next step of this process, which is sleep itself.

After the last good night kiss, the smiling little sleepover guest was tucked neatly away beneath the covers. The evening had proven to be all that Grandma had dreamed it would be. Apparently, only the smiley-face pancakes for breakfast in the morning remained as the grand finale for this romantic scrapbook event.

An instruction manual with a contractual agreement should be printed, read, and signed (this should definitely include Grandpa's signature) by all parties considering such an event. Without such a manual, we found ourselves, or should I say Grandpa found himself, unprepared for some of the minor details that would become part of the sleepover process. It was also obvious that Jadis had never had access to such a manual and became very confused with the order and timing that would constitute a successful sleepover.

At 1:30 a.m., something in Jadis's subconscious informed her that her surroundings were not what she was accustomed to. In her confused state of mind, it seemed like the time to explore the house. Perhaps her mother was here somewhere and had chosen this moment to engage in game of hide-and-seek. Evidently, Jadis had determined that the hiding period should be at an end and began calling out loudly for her missing mother to appear, perhaps to play another round. This loud calling out for missing persons is the cue for grandmothers to search for misplaced sleepers. Upon discovering Jadis in some distant portion of the house, it was determined that the original plan be somewhat altered to include sleeping in the same bed with Grandpa and Grandma.

Without a vote taken and agreed upon by all parties concerned, the decision was made to include a third sleeper directly in the center of our two-person bed. (When this missing manual can actually be completed, there should be considerable discussion on the legalities of such a move without the consent of all parties involved.)

Only moments into this new arrangement, it became evident that this event called sleep had not been appropriately named. If I recall correctly, the definition is *a natural, periodic state of rest for the mind and body, in which the eyes usually close and consciousness is completely or partially lost, so that there is a decrease in bodily movement and responsiveness to external stimuli.* Very little that took place after modifying our sleeping arrangement could even remotely qualify for this condition known as sleep.

I am not sure if five-year-olds lie motionless in this new, central strategic position for a few moments to cause their grandparents—that at this point have become unsuspecting victims—to conclude that all is now OK, or if they are really plotting their course for the next few hours. I think it was around 1:44 a.m. (requiring only about fourteen minutes to engage this new plan) that the people on either side of Jadis were well on their way to resuming a condition known as sleep. At this moment, Jadis chose to put the next portion of her plan into action. Somewhere in her subconscious she must have felt deprived of going for a walk or running in the park. Consequently, her feet and legs went into motion. At first she seemed to be just taking a quiet stroll, but without warning the motions changed to a frantic foot race. No doubt Jadis had taken on one of the characters from a Bible story she had just heard Grandma read before bed.

Jadis was very good about keeping her eyes closed through-out the activity, from start to finish, which is the only part of the sleep definition that she remotely qualified for. Evidently, Jadis

127

concluded that her grandpa's legs and feet were sufficiently bruised from the frantic foot race that she had just completed. She paused momentarily, taking a short break in the action, again providing a false sense of security and hope for some rest for the remaining portion of the night.

At 1:56 a.m., this time with just a twelve-minute pause, Jadis remembered another of her bedtime stories that needed to be reenacted. The picture of Samson pushing on those massive pillars in the Philistine temple no doubt left an indelible impression on her young mind; a vivid reenactment would be the next phase of our early morning grandparenting experience. Without warning, those little arms became taut and rigid, with one bracing against Lesa on one side, and me on the other, pushing with superhuman strength. The laws of physics were definitely being challenged. The object with the most mass and density was the one being forced from the bed. The smaller object lying peacefully on the other side of the bed from little Sampson seemed to be unaffected. As I felt this unbelievable force transporting my body in the direction of the edge, I was totally mystified. It was an absolute impossibility that such a small source of power could be responsible for such a maneuver. So much for equal and opposite reactions that our science books promised could be counted on. I wonder if the Philistines were as surprised by this impossible feat as I. If this were somehow a perfect reenactment, perhaps only one of the pillars actually collapsed, and the other was simply a bracing point. The whole experience continued to be a mystery. I was being transported closer to the edge and as I felt I was about to fall off a high precipice, I opted to alter the conclusion to the Philistine story. Sitting up in bed, I somehow overpowered the mighty arms that had propelled me to the edge and a near fall. I returned Jadis to her central, neutral battle position, hoping there would be a degree of physical fatigue. Perhaps exhaustion would modify some of her remaining plans, allowing her to consider some real sleep.

Moments of silence and steady breathing can be a little deceiving and lead to a false sense of security, but this was the tactic that Jadis repeatedly engaged in as her regrouping mode. This time, my exhaustion caused me to enter a momentary state of rest. Jadis's next tactic was much more subtle. In what seemed like only moments, I awoke with the realization that my head was off the pillow and very close to falling off the bed. Putting my head back on my pillow, I knew I would need to reassess the situation and re-evaluate my position. With the moon providing some dim light, I was able to get a better view of this one-child tactical force that had invaded my bed.

Is it possible that someone can smile while asleep? The moonlight shining through the window provided just enough light to highlight Jadis's face. It was as if she were smiling at me, perhaps even gloating over her victory as the conqueror of my bed. This right of passage as a fully certified grandparent was a bit more costly than I had at first imagined. Faced with the decision of how to rectify the situation, or to begin planning my own strategy for the remainder of this battle, I scooped up my assailant, returning her to the central neutral zone once again. Afraid to reference the nearby clock for the remaining number of minutes of our little sleepover ceremony, I now lay wide awake, wondering what strategy would be next on my assailant's agenda.

I was not sure how many other stories Lesa may have read to Jadis that might yet remain on the reenactment list. Not to wait long, as Jadis's arm swung quickly in my direction with hand open wide, landing across my face. Perhaps she was keeping me from delivering an inappropriate message before a king or had some other noble reason for covering my mouth. I really couldn't be sure, but at this point I really hoped she was trying to save me, rather than finish me off. Now the facial bruises would match my whole lower body. In fact, there were few portions of my body left unscathed.

It came as no surprise that many other stories were yet to be enacted. The next story had to be the boy David winding up with his sling to take out the giant, Goliath. This maneuver successfully attacked the remaining portions of the midsection thus far unaffected. With my entire body covered with bruises and feeling beaten both physically and psychologically, I knew that to actually win this battle would mean forfeiture of my grandparent status.

Not desiring to know the reenactment of the rest of the stories that may come to Jadis' subconscious, I knew the time had come to raise the white flag by retreating to the living room couch. I couldn't help looking back one last time to see if my assailant, now conqueror, was still smiling in the dark as I slid out of bed to make my way to safety. In the dim light of our bedroom it was impossible to be certain, but it sure looked like she was smiling bigger than ever.

Making the march to the living room, much like a prisoner of war being driven to another destination, I passed through the bathroom. Glancing at the bathtub, I wondered if some of the swelling and bruising would go down if I filled the tub with ice and spent the rest of the night just chilling. Not knowing if I could survive any further trauma, I continued my march to the living room and the waiting couch.

In this safe place of retreat, I lay wide-awake, contemplating the cost of grandparenthood. I had never dreamed the test would cost so much, but I had passed the test!

For those of you who are yet uncertified grandparents, I urge you to prepare rigorously each day until the day finally arrives for your test. You will need all the preparation you can possibly get. You should know that those of us who are certified grandparents are listening as you loosely throw around the terms grandpa and grandma.

Our world is filled with children who experience only pain and suffering. I am so thankful that God knows not only Jadis' name but every child as well. While Jesus ministered on planet earth, He instructed His followers, "Suffer the little children to come unto Me" (Matt. 19:14). Won't you join me in loving a child for Jesus? Why not learn the names of the children who make up your world? Would you like to see a small child's eyes dance with joy? Call them by name, and you will observe a display of magic in their eyes. Let's join hands bringing little children to Jesus.

If the Creator of the vast universe filled with planets and stars came to this earth to hold small children on His lap, don't you think He knows your name as well?

JON

⟫⟩◉⟨⟪

H ey, Jonny! Run out to the mailbox and get the paper. I'll time you," his father challenged from his comfortable chair in the living room. Jon was lying on the living room floor watching TV with his brothers, Reggie and Robbie, and his two sisters, Lesa and Kristi. His mother, Ellen, paused from her supper cleanup long enough to look through the doorway into the living room to observe Jon considering the challenge of racing to the mailbox.

Knowing that his family was smiling in anticipation, he could not resist the thought of winning a contest, even though he was the only competitor. He had been enticed many times before to attempt a new record while his father relaxed comfortably in his favorite chair.

Jon was a born competitor. If the family was hoeing in the field, he made sure he was first to complete his row. If they were baling hay, Jon figured out the fastest way to do it. Anyone who did not measure up to his pace would be considered a slacker. Though Jon was the youngest of the boys in the family, he could never be mistaken for a pushover when it came to any sort of contest. He just had to win

"Jon, I'm timing you. One, two, three," called out the officiator of the event. After only a moment's hesitation Jon leaped to his feet, racing for the door like he had been shot out of a cannon. In a flash he bolted back into the house with the evening paper, panting as he requested his latest time from the official timekeeper.

The Nelsons were a family of born athletes. Rodger, Jon's dad, had been a very impressive competitor all his life. From the time they were young he inspired his sons to be the best they could be. As the Nelson boys grew older, all of them loved playing football in the front yard of the huge white farmhouse. Reggie, the oldest, blessed with the most muscular build, received state recognition as one of the best high school football players in his division. Jon, Robbie, and Reggie each became serious wrestlers, competing all the way to the level of state competition.

Jon and Robbie never lost their love for playing softball. Slow pitch or fast, it didn't matter. After completing high school, Jon played in every softball tournament he could enter. He played the shortstop position nearly flawlessly. It was very difficult to hit anything between second and third base without seeing Jon go sailing through the air with his body fully extended, snagging a ball that should not have been caught.

Jon also enjoyed bowling during the long Wisconsin winter months that prohibited him from outdoor sports. He was just as much a favorite for those making up teams for bowling leagues as he was for the softball teams. More often than not, Jon would exceed 200 pins in each of the three games played in league competition. With Jon's reputation, his phone was always ringing with an invitation to bowl.

Even Jon's two sisters, Lesa and Kristi, were competitive in sports offered to girls. With their brothers excelling in nearly every sport, it seemed natural to become cheerleaders during their high school years, making the whole family involved in one way or another. Ellen, their mom, enjoyed golfing and bowling in couples leagues, as well as drawing the lot of chauffeur, busing her little team of athletes from event to event. As you can see, the Nelson family was serious about sports.

The Nelson family followed the Lutheran tradition, passed down for generations, attending church fairly regularly. Rodger's grandfather had been a circuit-riding preacher in the early days, covering a number of small towns in his area.

As Jon entered his teen years, he had less and less time for church and God. Socializing and parties engaged more and more of his time and attention. An early marriage to Bonnie, one of his high school sweethearts, dissolved rather quickly, separating him from his beautiful little daughter, Teena. Somewhat disillusioned with a broken relationship, he found himself back in the fast lane once again. For the next few years Jon worked as a carpenter by day and a partier by night.

After a few years of single life, Jon began to pursue a serious relationship with Sherri, also from Stoughton. They soon married and settled into a routine. Two fun-loving boys, Blaze and Dylan, joined Jon and Sherri not long into their marriage.

Jon continued working as a carpenter for Miller Construction in Madison. He engaged in his carpentry work just as he had every other part of his life, making work a contest to see how quickly he could complete a task without compromising on quality. What employer wouldn't like to have such a pacesetter on his job? Jon also had a good eye for detail and quickly became a favorite with Miller Construction. Receiving several promotions and raises, Jon's future looked bright and promising.

Blaze and Dylan were now getting old enough that Jon could really have fun with them. In the evenings he began to teach them to play ball. He looked forward to coming home to play with his boys. Jon couldn't wait to start coaching them in the sports he loved.

One evening, coming home tired from a long day at work, all Jon wanted was to relax with his family and enjoy the peaceful surroundings of their country home. Blaze and Dylan greeted him with an enthusiastic welcome as only energetic preschoolers can. After a little tussle and a few hugs, the family sat down to enjoy a nice evening meal together. Blaze and Dylan had many important details to share with Dad as they ate. The ring of the telephone created a pause in the conversation.

"I'll answer it," Sherri said, looking over at Jon with his fork motion.

As Sherri walked to the phone, Jon called to her with a last minute request. "If it's for me, tell them I'm not home."

Sherri instantly recognized the voice on the other end of the line. "Hello, Rex. How can I help you?" After listening for a moment, Sherri replied, "He said to tell you he's not home."

After another brief conversation, Sherri consented to pass the phone to Jon. He got up from the table, mumbling about never being able to just enjoy an evening at home with his family. He was quite certain he already knew what his friend Rex, captain of a bowling team, might be calling about. He had called Jon several other evenings when his team was scheduled to bowl. Answering the phone Jon said, "Forget it. I'm not going," without even hearing the appeal he knew would be coming. After listening for only a moment, Jon reinforced his position. "I'm tired tonight. I don't feel like bowling, and I'm not leaving the house. Why don't you call Rick?" After another word or two Jon hung up, returning to his half-eaten supper.

Blaze and Dylan were glad their dad was too tired to bowl tonight. They loved the thought of a whole evening with him. With only another bite or two from his plate eaten, the ringing of the telephone halted the conversation once again. With a disgusted look on his face, Jon slid his chair away from the table. Picking up the phone, he held to his initial position, clearly informing Rex that he was not interested in bowling. Jon then went on to supply a rather lengthy list of other possible candidates who might fill the vacancy on Rex's bowling team.

Hanging up, Jon returned to the table feeling like the issue had been sufficiently clarified. He was not going bowling tonight! With the bowling matter settled, Jon sat down to finish his supper, now growing colder by the minute. Relaxing with his family after finishing his meal, the phone rang again.

With disgust in his voice, he addressed the caller with an impatient, "Hello." As Jon listened in silence for the next few minutes, his family knew their evening together was on the line. With a weary sigh, Jon agreed to sub for Rex's missing bowler, and hung up. "He says tonight is really important. If they have to forfeit, their standings will really fall. He has tried everyone that he can think of, and either they aren't home or they have other plans."

Feeling frustrated, tired, and disgusted, one very unenthusiastic bowler bid his family goodbye and left for town. Arriving at the bowling alley feeling somewhat negative, he found his friends waiting for him.

"Hey, Nelson, glad you could help us out tonight," welcomed one of the waiting bowlers.

"Sure, no problem," Jon replied with a sarcasm that couldn't be missed.

"Jon, come on. Loosen up! We're going to have a good time. I think you need a shot of Jack Daniels to help you get with the program," encouraged Rex, as he put a shot of whiskey and a beer in front of Jon.

Jon took his seat, and the night was on. Rex had a very competitive team, and with Jon's help they were doing well. The only thing to do when you are winning is celebrate. And celebrate they did, with more whiskey and more beer. With their exuberant celebrating, it became apparent they were going to have a little difficulty with the last game. One of the team members, coming prepared for just such an emergency, had brought enough cocaine for the whole team! A quick trip outside to do a little coke, and they were ready for action once again. The cocaine gave everyone the lift they needed to get back on track. After the game, more celebrating seemed appropriate. With another trip or two outside for a little more coke, the evening was complete. It was very late by the time any of the heavily intoxicated bowlers remembered they still needed to find their way home.

Bidding the other heroes of the night goodbye, Jon made his way to his waiting pickup. The cold winter air momentarily provided a degree of sobriety. Jon had several miles of winding country road to negotiate between the bowling alley and his farmhouse. Aiming his truck at the right hand side of the road, he headed for home. The drive home began fairly routinely, but as the heater began to change the temperature from cold to comfortably warm, drowsiness set in. Just minutes from home, Jon's eyes closed as he drove down the dark country road. In an instant he was jolted back to consciousness by the sound of gravel pelting the underside of his cab. He had drifted off the road and down the sloping shoulder into the ditch. Realizing that he needed to get back onto the road, he gave the steering wheel a hard jerk, causing the truck to veer sharply to the left. As the oversized tires, sliding sideways through the gravel, caught the pavement, the pickup began to roll repeatedly. When the rolling truck finally came to rest he was in a farmer's front yard.

"Oh, great! I wrecked my truck," Jon moaned as it came to rest right side up with the motor still running. It took a moment or two to regain orientation in the darkness after bouncing and rolling around for such a long distance. He realized he had ended his circular tumble sprawled out across the seat. Looking around the cab in the dim moonlight, he searched for the ignition key to shut off his engine. He certainly did not want his crash to end in an explosion. As Jon attempted to reach for the key, his body did not respond. He could not move. The sudden realization that he was paralyzed caused a wave of terror and panic to sweep over him. Never before had he experienced such a feeling of total helplessness. The reality that the truck he was lying in could at any moment become an inferno was horrifying. The thought of Blaze and Dylan facing the future without their dad only heightened his fear and panic. The more he contemplated Blaze and Dylan with no one to enjoy their ball games, no one to teach them to wrestle and do all the things he had been waiting to experience with them, the more he knew he had to live. Waiting alone in the darkness Jon called out to the God he had known as a boy, "I don't want to die."

After what felt like an eternity, Jon heard the wail of sirens coming closer and closer. In another moment the sky around him appeared to be pulsating with flashing red lights and voices of firefighters moving in to stabilize the crash site and begin the process of removing him from the tangled mass of metal. Jon felt himself being slid onto a backboard. As the emergency medical technicians began to evaluate his condition, it became evident that a severe spinal injury would necessitate an airlift to a trauma center in Madison, Wisconsin. Before long Jon heard the rhythm of the approaching helicopter and the Med-flight team quickly loaded him for transport to the trauma center.

Our family was living in the Dominican Republic when Lesa received an emergency message that her brother Jon had been in a serious accident. Traveling as quickly as possible, we hurried to the nearest phone to learn the details. After a brief description of the accident, Lesa was informed that Jon was paralyzed, but it was still too soon to know what his condition would be after his body stabilized from the trauma. With tickets already purchased for our family's return home in a couple of months, Lesa was encouraged not to make any changes to her plans for the moment. If something should develop, she would be notified. All the family could do was wait and pray that God would stay near Jon. Time seemed to stand still for Lesa as she thought of her brother lying a hospital bed.

As soon as Lesa arrived home, she hurried to the hospital to visit Jon. Approaching the information desk at the hospital, she asked the attendant for directions to Jon Nelson's room. With a prayer in her heart, she stepped into the elevator. Jon was on a floor specializing in neurological care. When Lesa reached Jon's room, the privacy curtain was drawn. She could not see who was in the bed behind the curtain.

"Jonny?" Lesa called to the other side of the curtain.

The voice of a nurse from behind the curtain responded rather abruptly, "Don't come in here! I will let you know when I am finished."

"Oh, I'm sorry. I'll wait here until you're finished," Lesa quietly responded.

From behind the curtain came a very soft voice, "Hi, Les."

Hearing the voice of the brother she had been longing to hug and comfort caused a wave of emotion to sweep over her. Finally the moment had come to be reunited with her brother and soul mate from childhood. It was all she could do to fight back the floodgate holding her tears. Her emotions had been welling up inside for several long weeks. Knowing that Jon had never cared for tears reminded Lesa she just had to hold it all in for the time being. Jon would surely mistake tears of heartache for tears of sympathy or pity. Growing up, tears had been associated with weakness. The only thing left to do was continue to fight back the tears and be strong. The moments of waiting with just a curtain separating them seemed like an eternity.

Rather matter-of-factly the nurse pulled back the curtain and walked out of the room, leaving Jon and Lesa alone for a painful reunion. Walking over to the bed, Lesa repeated her greeting, this time looking deep into his eyes, attempting to understand the cry of his heart. Reaching the bed she took his lifeless hand and gave him a kiss on the cheek. How she longed for the opportunity to lift him into her arms for the kind of embrace that would more adequately let him feel the love she wanted so desperately to communicate. Looking into Jon's eyes it was not difficult to see that he was having an equally challenging moment with emotions that were just beneath the surface. If only it were OK to cry!

After their initial greetings, Jon said with a hidden excitement and a new strength in his voice, "Lesa, there is a God."

"I know Jon," Lesa replied with a smile.

As if he were trying to will her to understand something far beneath the surface, he reiterated his declaration a second time, "No. I mean there IS a God." As he repeated his words with earnestness too big to miss, it became clear that something had taken place that had made a profound impact on his life.

Lesa was anxious to discover the reason for this bold statement so out of character for a brother. He always avoided the topic of God. Responding to his earnest statement Lesa inquired, "*I know, but why are you saying that?*"

Jon had been waiting to share his amazing answer with his sister whom he knew had been praying for him for many years. As he began his explanation, the expression on his face and the look of excitement in his eyes clearly indicated he was reliving a portion of the accident that Lesa had not yet heard. Jon began to replay the scenes that had led up to that fateful night and what would be his last drive home. He relived his experience in his pickup as it rolled over and over, and the sensation of his body bouncing from objects in every part of the cab. As the realization that this was not just a nightmare but reality, the thought of never watching his boys learn to play ball, never watching them learn to do all the things he had dreamed of teaching them, was more than he could bear. Overwhelmed with the inability to move in his helpless condition and the possibility of his life ending in such a meaningless way, he cried out into the blackness of the night to the God he had walked away from many years earlier.

"I don't want to die!"

Silently he asked for the privilege of life with his boys, though he could tell he was paralyzed. Reaching this point of his story a new earnestness and excitement shone through his voice as he searched for just the right words to sufficiently portray the scene that was so vivid in his mind.

"Although I had bounced to every portion of the cab, my body came to rest lying across the truck seat," Jon continued. "Lesa, God came to the seat I was lying on. He lay down face-to-face right in front of me. His whole being radiated a peace and love. Even though it was pitch black outside, the whole cab became illuminated with a brilliant light. I could read every number and letter of the instruments on the dash. I felt a warm calm come in place of the panic and fear I had just been feeling. As He looked at me with those eyes of love, He said, 'It's going to be all right Jon. You're not going to die.' He waited with me for several minutes and then vanished. The brilliant light of His presence lingered for a few minutes before the cab became dark once again. But His presence, surrounding me with a calm and peace, remained even as the paramedics removed me from the truck and the Med-flight team flew me to the hospital."

Still tracing the outline of his limp and lifeless hand, and with earnestness that matched Jon's penetrating gaze, Lesa pondered the amazing picture of God she had just heard. After a moment of deep silence Lesa responded, "That sounds like God."

Lying motionless, Jon continued his case for God's existence. "As I lay in my hospital bed slowly recovering from the trauma of the accident I dreaded with each passing day the moment I would have to face Blaze and Dylan. I knew it wouldn't be long before the inevitable reunion. How could I let them see me like this? I'm supposed to be the one to take care of them. I would not even be able to reach out and hug them as they came to see me. Feelings of helplessness bombarded me. The more I thought about it the more depressed and fearful I felt. Finally the day I was dreading more than any other since my accident came. I really didn't think I would be able to handle the heartbreak and pain." Fixing his eyes once again on Lesa, Jon continued with a renewed sincerity, "Lesa, He came back again. Just before my boys came through the door, Jesus came and lay in the bed beside me with His arm around my neck and shoulders. All the peace and calm I felt in the truck that night came back again. He stayed for the entire visit, lying with His arm around me as I talked with Blaze and Dylan, Mom, Dad and Sheri." Charged with emotion, Jon stared in silence once again into the eyes of his sister whom he knew would appreciate the picture of the wonderful Savior he had just shared.

Many years have passed since that fateful night on a country road that changed Jon's life forever. Jon has courageously pressed forward with his dream to be a father to his two boys. Though he spends his days confined to a wheelchair, he remains thankful for the gift of life and the opportunity to see his boys grow up.

Not long ago Jon wrote a poem that powerfully speaks to all who will listen. I would like to include this poem as the conclusion to his story.

Note: words that might need clarification in his poem...

Jack—Jack Daniels whiskey
Blow—using cocaine
Cokin' —using cocaine
Tokin' —smoking marijuana or cocaine
Crosses—amphetamines

Drinkin' an' Tokin'

Jack and Beer
A little Blow
Hop in the car
Off I go
Drivin' Fast
Happens when your Cokin'
Wasted Life Drinkin' an' a Tokin'
Wasted life Drinkin' an' a Tokin'
Cost me 2 wives an' a couple of kids
Can't believe soma the things that I did
The folks I hurt and the ones I let down
It's been 10 years since my feet hit the ground
Hands Hang
Legs of lead
Many a day
Wish I was dead
Body lost
Neck broken
Wasted life Drinkin' an' a Tokin'
Wasted life Drinkin' an' a Tokin'
Handful of Crosses as I try to get by
I look in the mirror and I wonder why
The eyes are dead but in the lines I see
I spent my whole life just thinkin' of me
Close book
On Life that I own
Realize
It's all been on loan
50 years since my eyes were 'woken
Wasted 'em all
Drinkin' an' a Tokin'
Wasted 'em all
Drinkin' an' a Tokin'

As you behold the demonstration of matchless love from the Savior of man, interrupting the affairs of the universe to calm the fears of one of His children who had repeatedly spurned His gift of life, can you help but wonder who could resist such a God filled with a love so infinite? Is it any wonder that the redeemed of all ages will praise His gift of amazing grace throughout the ceaseless ages of eternity? What a thrill as we compare story with story! I can't wait to hear yours!

If the Creator of the vast universe filled with planets and stars could hear the cry of anguish and despair from a wounded son who had run fast and hard from one entreaty after another, don't you think He knows your name as well?

ROZANNA

Note—this story not recommended for children

I would like to invite Rozanna to introduce her story. I believe her words form a powerful appeal for those of us living in a world being bombarded with spiritual darkness.

Come with me on a journey into my past. Many things which I will share may seem far-fetched or a figment of an over-active imagination. But it is my prayer that, if you are not able to identify with my story, or if it seems unrealistic to you, you will continue to be protected by the Holy Spirit and appreciate and value the shadow of the Savior's protecting wings.

> *I share my testimony to emphasize what impact right or wrong choices can have on our lives and the lives of our families. I am alarmed at how modern it has become to go to palm readers, to make movies on witchcraft targeted at teenagers, and to write books on the occult and witchcraft in good fun. There is a very thin line between these two worlds, and I believe that we should be aware of them, of their power, and that under no circumstances, should they be given a foothold into our lives—not through books, not through movies, not through games! Once they do, it*

is very difficult to disentangle oneself, and only through prayer and divine intervention can one hope to be set free.

Rozanna looked longingly from her front yard at the other children playing up and down the street. The jubilant laughter of boys and girls her age echoing through the neighborhood mocked her loneliness. They played games, ran through the park, and sat in small groups sharing the latest developments in the world of six-year-olds.

"Why can't I play with the other children? What's wrong with me?" wondered little Rozanna. Watching two of the neighbor girls playing skip rope, as they call it in South Africa, made her feel even worse. "Why do all the white people hate us so much? What have we done?" queried the heart of a lonely little girl pondering the injustices of the world around her. "I will just have to go in the house and ask Mum. It just isn't fair," Rozanna thought as she walked up to her front door.

The soft, beautiful voice of her mother singing lifted her spirits. Her music made the bitterness of rejection not sting quite as much. "I am so glad that my mum always sings. I think she must have the most beautiful voice in the whole world," Rozanna thought as she neared her mother working in the kitchen.

"How's my little girl this afternoon?" inquired Rozanna's mother as she rested her spoon on the edge of the large bowl she was stirring. "What's that long face all about?"

"It's not fair that I can't play with the other kids just because they are white! Why do people spit at us and call out terrible names when we walk down the street? Why can't I go to school like all the other kids?" began the heartbroken inquiry. "Sometimes I wish we did not live in this big house in our rich neighborhood with all these nice things if it means I can't even play! Will it always be like this?" Rozanna sighed.

Silently looking into the eyes of her little girl, Marguarita longed for an encouraging word to share, but there was none. How could she explain something called apartheid, with all the official government policies defining radical racial discrimination, when it didn't make sense to her? How could she explain that those in government believed they were a superior race? What reason could she give Rozanna for not belonging in the same restaurants, stores, and schools as white girls? What could she possibly say that would heal her wounded heart? Holding Rozanna tightly in her arms she could only whisper, "I don't know." The icy stares and cutting comments caused her to feel the same lonely, isolated feelings her daughter was experiencing. Something would surely happen soon. Life simply could not go on like this.

Marguarita was an attractive native South African gifted with a beautiful voice and nimble fingers on the piano. It had not taken long for the entertainment world to discover a voice that could bring back the crowds at the most elite and prestigious nightclubs in town.

A Greek businessman who had recently immigrated to South Africa came into the club where Marguarita was singing one night. As her sweet melody charmed the listeners, he became captivated with her voice and graceful mannerisms. Night after night drew him back to the clubs where Marguarita performed. He wanted this beautiful woman for his wife and set his business mind to accomplish the task. Sitting alone with Marguarita after a performance one evening, he invited her to share the rest of her life with him. He promised to love and care for her with the best that money could buy. Looking into her beautiful dark eyes he said, "I want you to be the mother of my children."

His plan sounded too good to be true. Marguarita had to make a difficult choice. She had just been offered an attractive contract with a recording studio in the United Kingdom. Her career as a vocalist would be assured. Her future looked bright with promise.

"Don't leave me," pleaded her new admirer. "I will make your life better than all the fame and fortune you could gain in the United Kingdom."

After much thought, Marguarita chose the love of her Greek businessman. They were soon married and began to live the life of dream and promise. They purchased a home in one of the prestigious developments in their city.

A business opportunity came along not long after their marriage that required a substantial investment. With a little financial assistance, their family business opportunities would be limitless. Marguarita's savings from her musical career became the needed investment to take her husband's enterprise to the next level. The future looked bright with promise.

A beautiful baby girl named Rozanna came soon, fulfilling the first part of their dream. A new dimension of happiness was added to Marguarita's life as she watched Rozanna learn to walk and talk. Marguarita loved to play the piano and sing for her little girl. Rozanna became the audience to appreciate the voice that had been destined for recording. Marguarita didn't seem to mind the loss of her musical dream. She was happy, and life was good.

The neighbors and business associates were anything but happy. A stranger had immigrated to South Africa with blatant disregard for their laws. He had married a black woman, which was not just considered unethical, it was illegal. A stranger would not be allowed to erode their culture. He would be dealt with!

Rozanna awoke with a start. Loud banging on the front door and angry voices demanding entrance caused her to sit up in bed. She could faintly hear her father talking to the men at the front door. "What could be the matter?" she wondered. Peering out her bedroom window she watched as group of police officers pushed past her father, making their way to her parents' bedroom. In horror she watched her mother being dragged from bed in the arms of the local police. Marguarita was being arrested for an act defined by South African law as immoral. Since any marriage between a white man and a black woman was considered invalid, sleeping with her husband was considered committing an immoral act.

Rozanna was terrified, watching her mother disappear into the night. "What are they going to do with my mum?" wailed little Rozanna to her father.

"You just wait here. I will go down to the police station and straighten this all out," Rozanna's father said, attempting to comfort his daughter.

Her mother and father returned that night, but everything began to change. Night after night the police would come, dragging her mother from bed and down to the police station, demanding enormous fines from a businessman they knew could afford to pay. Threatened with the ruin of his business, deportation back to Greece, and jail for his wife, he felt forced to make some new arrangements. He purchased another large house on the other side of town from him and his business, with the agreement that he would come and visit Rozanna and her mother once a week. He would bring them food and supplies, while he stayed and maintained their present home until all this could be straightened out.

Rozanna's world had just been turned upside down. She was living in a new house with very few furnishings. Something about this new house did not feel good to her. She missed having Mum and Dad in the same house. Each week her dad would come with food and stay for a visit, but it wasn't the same. The sad look on her mother's face each time her father left made her feel sad, too. The warm hugs and kisses she used to see between her them had faded away as well. Nothing felt the same.

"Rozanna, you watch your dad for me. If he starts to wake up, wave your hand and I will come back in before he sees that I am looking through his car," instructed Rozanna's mother. "Your dad has been acting differently for quite awhile now. I want to see if I can find anything in his car that will help me find out what is going on," Rozanna's mother whispered as she slipped out the door.

Rozanna felt frightened. She watched her father sleeping across the room and her mother searching frantically through the car outside. Her heart skipped a beat as her father's sleeping form stirred and sighed before resuming restful breathing. As Rozanna continued her vigilant watch, she could see that her mother was sobbing. Marguarita slowly walked back to the house, carrying a handful of intimate pictures from one of the female employees at her husband's firm. In her other hand she held a stack of handwritten letters confirming her dreaded suspicions.

Confronted with the letters and pictures, her husband flew into a rage. "You had no right to invade the privacy of my car," screamed the man who had always been so kind. He was the man who everyone in town knew to be a perfect gentleman. "I'll teach you to get into my stuff!" With a clenched fist he smashed Marguarita in the face, sending her flying across the room nearly unconscious.

"Leave my mum alone!" Rozanna screamed in horror, running to her mother's bruised and broken body. "Get out of here!"

Rozanna watched the man she had always loved as her father pause for one last, long evil stare and then walk out the door as a mad man. Never again would she know the warmth of her father's love.

The regular weekly visits with food became sporadic visits without any food or supplies. Without warning, Rozanna's father would burst through the door just for the pleasure of beating his helpless wife. Smashing his fist into her helpless frame over and over again, he would scream, "Where is your God? Why does He not help you? Where is your God?" He had become a raging demon with a vengeance against his family and God.

Words can not portray the brokenness and heartbreak of watching your father trying to kill your mother before your eyes. How can the horror of watching your father trying to suffocate your mother be understood? First he shoved his entire fist into her mouth to keep her from breathing. After a few moments her limp body crumpled to the floor. Attempting to snuff out any remaining life he sat on her head with a pillow. Each time he returned, it seemed that he became more enraged. Frustrated with his failure to end the life of his helpless wife, he would storm out the door.

Little Rozanna was only seven years old when the beatings and cursing of her mother's God became her father's routine. What had happened to the love in her father? Rozanna would run to her mother's side, hoping to intervene in her behalf, but it was no use. Her father was a giant of a man, and her mother a petite woman with a seven-year-old daughter as her only defense. After several attempted interventions, Rozanna was locked in another room as her mother was mercilessly beaten, to prevent her from interfering in his acts of raging madness. It was after one of these terrible beatings, as Rozanna's mother lay near death on the floor, that her father further violated her brokenness by forcing himself on her as a final insult to her dignity. As a result, a little brother joined their pain-filled family.

Rozanna's mother was totally helpless. There was no such thing as a shelter for her to flee to. Apartheid was at its peak, meaning government aid of any kind would be impossible. Her family had abandoned her for marrying a white man. She had little education, and had invested all her savings into the family business. She was totally dependent on a husband who had forgotten the meaning of love.

Marguarita needed help desperately, but where could she go? She believed in God and took her children to church. She taught her children to pray and worship; she taught them to respect and care for others, as God would have us to. She taught her children to read the Bible, but never fully understood the power it contained. She knew of Jesus, but had never known the joy of a full surrender to Him and the power that follows.

Marguarita began to look in all the wrong places for power and strength. In South Africa, voodoo and witchcraft are familiar sources of supernatural power that have entrenched themselves into the culture and society for centuries.

"Come along, Rozanna. We are going to the witch doctor today. He will help us win your father back," Rozanna's mother said as she prepared for the long walk across town.

Walking to the outskirts of town, Rozanna and her mother turned down a long, winding pathway leading to a house with many strange objects displayed about the yard. Stepping into the darkened room, Rozanna and her mother walked toward the witch doctor as he motioned for them to sit in front of him. Rozanna's eyes grew large as she inspected the many bottles filled with strange contents, creature parts, and numerous abominable liquids. Horrible smells insulted their nostrils. Rozanna's stomach felt queasy as she tried to breathe without smelling at the same time. The witch doctor listened intently as Marguarita sadly detailed her need for power to win back her husband.

The witch doctor rose and began to utter strange incantations, ranting and raving to the spirits and gods. Lighting a foul substance that smoldered in the darkness, he began to pray over Rozanna and her mother as he moved about the room. Finishing his prayer, he took one of the bottles from the wall. Slowly he poured some of the contents into two small glasses, instructing both Rozanna and her mother to drink it.

Rozanna's nose recoiled as she drew the glass close to her mouth. Her already queasy stomach began to churn and roll in anticipation of the concoction about to enter her body. Touching the glass to her lips, Rozanna bravely began to swallow the contents of the glass. The putrid smell did not make the swallowing an easy process as pieces of floating objects slid across her tongue and down her throat. It was all she could do to keep her stomach from sending the contents back the way it had come. In a state of nausea, Rozanna and her mother made their exit with the promise of power in their behalf.

In desperation, Rozanna's mother returned over and over to various witch doctors, Repeatedly, she was instructed to drink abominable potions. The promised power never came. When it became clear that the witch doctors could not help, the voodooists were sought after. In search of power, a whole new approach to appeasing the spirits took place. Over and over Rozanna's and her mother's skin was slashed in ritual ceremonies so evil spirits would be warded off. Leaving weak and faint, with blood still oozing from their wounds, they made their way home. Each failed attempt left Marguarita feeling more desperate and hopeless. Rozanna was required to accompany her mother back and forth from witch doctor to voodooist.

As they visited a witch doctor one day, he informed Marguarita that the young lady who had become her husband's mistress had sought out a very powerful spirit medium, seeking her destruction. Her husband had lied to the young girl, telling her he could not marry her because his wife had threatened to kill herself if he did. Consequently, this young lady employed the most powerful witch doctor she could find to remove the barrier separating her from her desired wedding.

The validity of the words of the witch doctor became apparent almost immediately. Not long after learning of her dreaded fate, the oppressive spirits began their work. While Marguarita and her children were sleeping in the middle of the night, the sound of someone knocking at the back door awakened everyone in the house.

"Mummy, who is trying to get in our kitchen door?" Rozanna called out in the dark.

"Quiet! It must be someone trying to break into our house," Marguarita whispered to her children. Calling them to her bedroom, Marguarita locked the door to protect her family the best she could in the event that the would-be thief was able to gain access to their home. Breathlessly they crouched in the dark, waiting to see what would happen. Finally the knocking stopped.

The next day they began their investigation of the doors and windows to see what might have been happening the night before. After searching for a clue to the visitor the night before, they gave up. There was no evidence of any foul play.

Exhausted from the sleepless night before, Marguarita tucked her children in bed early. Once again, in the middle of the night the knocking began. Feeling alone in their big empty house without any protection intensified their apprehension. What or who could be knocking? Too scared to sleep, they felt trapped in their home. Night after night the knockings persisted. As time went on, strange sounds began to come from inside the house. Sounds of plates crashing to the floor came from the kitchen. An eerie feeling of evil crept into their house night after night. In the mornings as the sun came up, the frightened trio gathered enough courage to come from behind locked doors. Walking from room to room, they would inspect the house for the damage that they had listened to the night before. It was always the same; not a plate or dish was out of place. Only the vivid memories of the previous night remained.

One night, waking with a start from a sound sleep, Rozanna heard someone calling her mother's name in the darkness. Next, she heard her name being called, and then her brother's. Terrified, they listened, motionless, frozen in fear, as a mysterious voice continued to call them each by name. It was clear that an evil presence was in their home.

Continued visits to the voodooist and witch doctors proved fruitless to end the visits. From this time on, spiritual harassment turned into physical struggles that became a desperate fight for life. Rozanna was now nine years old and fighting for her life in her own home!

The occasional, violent visits from Rozanna's father could be heard and observed throughout the neighborhood, causing total alienation from the neighbors. From time to time he screamed at the top of his lungs, like a mad man, causing anyone within hearing to move to a safe haven. On one such outburst of rage, he began to attack Marguarita brutally. Fearing for her life, she ran barefoot into the street in an attempt to escape. The children playing skip rope in the street could instantly see what was taking place, as Marguarita dashed between them in an attempt to make her way to freedom. Rozanna felt humiliated beyond description as she encountered the other children of the neighborhood. No wonder the children had been instructed to stay clear of everyone in her house.

Further complicating their acceptance was the issue of color. Once again they were in an elite neighborhood that wanted nothing to do with them. The neighbors began an all-out initiative seeking their eviction. This family didn't fit their criteria as noble citizens. The neighbors called the police, stating that Marguarita was selling drugs out of her home. They quickly responded by forcing their way into the house, searching every square inch for hidden drugs. Finding nothing, the police left, warning Marguarita of the consequences of selling drugs and that they would be watching her. As if someone had erected a black flag over their yard identifying the residents as targets for scorn, both young and old began a vigilant campaign of taunting and jeering.

"Rozanna, I need you to run to the market for me," called her mother one afternoon. "I have a small list of things that you will be able to carry home with you."

After carefully reviewing the list, she opened the door, calling back to her mother, "I'll be back in a few minutes." Rozanna was nine now and loved going to the market for her mother. As she stepped into the street, a group of children playing nearby spotted her.

"Rozanna, where are you going? Mind if we come along?" called one of the neighbor boys who had been playing with a few of his friends across the street. The group of would-be friends began to whisper to each other as they approached Rozanna on her journey to the store.

"We just thought we would walk along with you, if you don't mind," one of the bigger boys said with a sneer. Smiling at the little band that was now tagging along beside him, he gave a little nod. With one last sneer the boy said, "Rozanna, we just want to be your friends."

Without warning, Rozanna felt a large glob of spit hit her in the face. The next thing she knew, her face was covered with spit coming from every side. With nowhere to hide, and unable to outrun all of them, she had to just keep on walking. After a few minutes they began to run out of saliva to hurl at their victim, ending the merciless attack.

Tears ran fast and free down Rozanna's cheeks as she walked along. Why did everyone hate her so? What had she done? The sting of her tears, the pokes and jabs as she walked along, being covered in spit, was more than she could endure. In fear and humiliation, Rozanna made her way to the market. Not daring to look up, she slowly shuffled her way back home. Carrying her small bag of groceries, her broken heart felt as though it would burst.

As she neared her yard, she heard the same sneering voice coming from behind some nearby bushes. "Rozanna, how fast can you run with your bag of groceries?"

Realizing her humiliation had not ended, Rozanna began to run as fast as she could, carrying her bag of groceries. Splat! The oozy slime of raw egg running down her hair spurred her on. Faster and faster the eggs came from all directions. As she leaped for the door, a final burst of eggs showered Rozanna and her house. With tears flowing freely once again, Rozanna, dripping in eggs, closed her front door, wishing she could shut away the awful jeers and laughter of the children outside.

Rozanna had nowhere to hide; the spirits of darkness terrorized her by night, and the neighbors terrorized her by day. Over and over she experienced abuse and insult from the neighbor children. They had chosen her as the object of relentless harassment.

In their darkest hour, God sent a kind lady named Frances Ross to the rescue. She picked up Marguarita and her children one Saturday morning, introducing them to a totally new, beautiful world: the Seventh-day Adventist Church in Plumstead, Cape Town, South Africa. For the first time in Rozanna's life no one asked her, "Are you white, or are you black?" For the first time in Rozanna's life, other children spoke to her and invited her to come and join them in their worship. Rozanna felt a flood of warmth and peace fill her soul, not only because she had experienced acceptance, but the adults had welcomed her mother in the same way. It was too good to be true—total strangers invited them to lunch.

These were the very first feelings of love and acceptance that Rozanna could ever remember feeling from persons outside of her family. The love and peace that radiated from the faces of the church members were as rays of warm sunshine on a cold, rainy day. This wounded family, beaten down on every side, felt like they had finally found a place to belong.

"Aunt Frances," as Rozanna called her, brought boxes of *Uncle Arthur's Bedtime Stories* and many other spiritual books. Week after week Aunt Frances and her husband, Albert, picked up Marguarita and her family to take them to church. These special people were the first ones to introduce Rozanna, her brother, and mother to Jesus. Aunt Frances brought her two sons when she went for visits just so Rozanna and her brother could actually play with other children. For the first time, laughter could be heard resounding throughout a house that was usually anything but joyful.

The nocturnal visits from the supernatural forces of darkness persisted throughout this time. Marguarita started to pray to the Jesus she had learned about; but the more she prayed, the worse things became. She continued to fight for her very life.

One night, at twelve o'clock exactly, seven tiny men appeared at her mother's bedside. As usual, Rozanna and her brother were awakened by their arrival. A chill of terror ran up Rozanna's spine as she heard them say, "Marguarita must die tonight."

Rozanna and her brother ran to the doorway watching helplessly as their mother battled with these demons of darkness. One by one the demons crawled up on Marguarita's bed, trying to force her mouth open so they could pour the contents of the bottle they had down her throat. Relentlessly they proceeded to carry out the death sentence they had been commissioned to fulfill.

Trembling in fear, Rozanna and her brother heard their mother cry out the name of Jesus. As she called on the name of Jesus, the demons wrestled her down, holding her tongue, so that the name of Jesus could not be uttered. Marguarita fought on and on. As the violent struggle neared the end, the room turned to a dark bluish color, terrifying the two young children beyond description. Just as suddenly as they had appeared, the demons were gone. From that night on Marguarita's health deteriorated slowly.

Despite having discovered a warm, loving church family, Marguarita was not able to totally place her trust in Jesus. She would attend church on Saturday and visit the witch doctors on Sunday. Her quest to find the most powerful and effective voodooist or witch doctor led Marguarita and her children into many dangerous places. Most of these spirit mediums lived on the outskirts of thick forests far from the cities.

On one of these walks, far from the city and deep inside a forest area, several men surrounded them. Their cold penetrating eyes left no doubt that these were dangerous men. The fate of anyone in their path could not be mistaken. As these men moved inward, encircling Rozanna and her mother, she felt the presence of Jesus encircle them as well. Although she could not see Him, she knew He was near. After inquiring where they were going, the entire group of hardened men turned and disappeared into the forest without even taking as much as Marguarita's purse.

The God that Rozanna was learning more and more about each week in church continued to demonstrate His love and protection. Twice, when Rozanna became lost in dangerous places, a girl about her age with a beautiful smile walked up to her, asking if she was lost and would she like help finding her way home. Without asking where Rozanna lived, this smiling girl led her back to her home. Turning to show her family who had walked her to safety, no one was there. The Jesus she was learning to know had surely sent an angel to guide her home.

One night as Rozanna's parents fought and argued, the spirits of darkness returned. As the argument continued to get louder and louder, three frogs, about three feet tall, wearing green sequined jackets and black top hats, appeared out of nowhere. They started jumping in perfect harmony up and down, laughing at Rozanna's fighting parents. The more her parents fought, the faster the frogs jumped, laughing and laughing at the two miserable individuals before them. Rozanna and her brother looked on fearfully from the other side of the room. As these incidents continued, Marguarita's health continued to deteriorate.

When Rozanna turned fourteen, they moved from the house with nightmares too numerous to count. Rozanna's father had met a young girl and finally left Marguarita in peace. Rozanna had never set foot in a school, as she was not accepted as a black in the black schools and not accepted as white in their schools. A group of Catholic sisters took pity on Rozanna, allowing her to begin school. It was a difficult task, beginning school at fourteen, trying to catch up to the others her age. With much persistence, Rozanna finally graduated from high school.

As her health deteriorated, God sent a kind Italian lady named Lorna to bless Marguarita and her family. She also loved Jesus, bringing joy and happiness with each of her visits. Her brother would stop by with groceries, not knowing that money for food had run out long before. God continued to demonstrate His love and watch care for this family so wounded and beaten down.

Marguarita continued to visit the witch doctors. In spite of Rozanna's pleading to just trust Jesus to heal her, she replied, "Jesus wants us to help ourselves, my child, and He will not be angry with me for seeking the help of the voodooist." Satan was lying to her, and she believed him.

In her illness one day, she began to vomit forks and knives. With a sense of evil all around, Rozanna and her brother looked on in silence. All Rozanna's pleading could not persuade her mother to turn to Jesus for help and healing. Six more years she lingered, balancing between life and death. At last her long life of pain and suffering came to an end. Marguarita closed her eyes, never more to suffer the cruel tyranny of the spirits of darkness. Rozanna and her brother would now finish life's course without her.

A few years later, Rozanna decided to leave South Africa for Europe, hoping she could find peace and happiness. Just a chance to live a normal life was all she desired. In Europe, an international company hired Rozanna for a very responsible position. The compensation was also very attractive, making possible the dream of the good life she had come in search of. She met a nice man who desired to share the rest of his life with her, and soon they were married. The dream she had left home and family for had come true, for the most part.

The God that Auntie Frances had introduced her to was no longer a part of her life. Somewhere along the way she had left Him behind. The Jesus who had spared her life over and over in her younger years and the friendship she had enjoyed with Him, was missing. Enjoying all the things prosperity and affluence provide had not been able to fill her heart with the peace that Jesus had once given.

In her emptiness, Rozanna called out to Jesus, asking Him to come into her life as her Savior and Lord. He answered her prayer, igniting within her a desire to serve Him completely. The occasional visitations from the spirits of darkness intensified greatly as Rozanna made the decision to make a full surrender to Jesus. The devil had claimed her as his own since she was a small girl with her mother, and he was not about to let her go. Rozanna prayed earnestly that God would deliver her from the tormenting spirits once and for all. The battle continued on and on. Rozanna began to fast and pray for God to lead her out of the terrible bondage that had tormented her life for so many years.

Feeling sick, Rozanna decided not to go in to work one day. Bored, just lying in bed, she decided to go downstairs and watch 3ABN (3 Angels Broadcasting Network) on television. The *3ABN Today* program had just begun with Shelly Quinn hosting an interview with a couple. They were describing a deliverance from the spirits of darkness as related in a book that they had recently published. As Rozanna continued listening to the interview, she heard the voice of God speak to her with explicit instructions: "Rozanna, you will find the answer you have been fasting and praying for in that book." At the conclusion of the program, Rozanna carefully noted the telephone number at the bottom of the screen to contact the guests who had just been interviewed.

"I don't know what time it is in the United States right now but I have to talk to these people," Rozanna thought. Picking up the phone she dialed the number.

"Who could be calling at this time of night?" Lesa wondered as she looked over at the alarm clock beside the bed displaying 2:00 a.m.

A long pause of silence was the only response to the "hello" she had offered to her late-night caller. After a few moments of silence, the buzz from the receiver signaled the retreat of her mystery caller. Hanging up with a sigh and hoping whoever had called had resolved their issue without any further need of assistance, she lay back down for some restful sleep. Almost as soon as her head returned to the pillow, the telephone rang again.

"Hello, is this Mrs. Budd?" began a faint voice at the other end.

Quite surprised that she was actually talking to a person making a legitimate phone call, Lesa said, "Yes, this is she."

"I'm sorry I don't know what time it is where you are. I am calling from Europe," continued the caller.

"That's OK. I wasn't sleeping anyway," Lesa replied.

"My name is Rozanna. I just finished watching your interview with Shelly Quinn on 3ABN and had to talk to you. I need one of Mr. Budd's books, *I Will Save You to Make You a Blessing*. I was sick today and decided not to go to work, even though I normally do.

I turned on 3ABN just as you began your interview. As you were describing your experience with demonic spirits and how God delivered you, God said to me, 'You will find the answer you have been fasting and praying for in that book.' Mrs. Budd, I have been fasting and praying for three weeks for deliverance from spiritual harassment. I grew up in a home with voodoo and witch doctors," Rozanna said.

In a weak and weary voice she sketched her troubled childhood and the harassment she had endured every since. "I believe Jesus can help me, don't you Mrs. Budd?" Rozanna said in a questioning voice.

"Yes, I do believe Jesus can set you free, and He will, too, but you must have faith and trust in His timing," Lesa began. "I don't know what you have in your house that the devil can claim as his property, but I am sure you will not experience freedom if you have any books, games, magazines, videos, music, or anything else the devil can claim as his."

After sharing some scriptures with promise and power for Rozanna's freedom, they prayed for God to lead in Rozanna's deliverance. Promising Rozanna she would continue to pray for her and be in touch by e-mail, Lesa returned the phone to the receiver. She continued to pray silently in the night for a new friend on the other side of the Atlantic who was obviously weary from a long battle with the forces of darkness.

Rozanna's e-mails continued to reveal a deepening relationship and surrender to Jesus. Her faith and trust in Jesus' power to deliver continued to grow with each passing day, although the spiritual battlefield had not abated in the least. In spite of the intense spiritual harassment, Rozanna praised God for the gifts of peace and grace that had been sustaining her even in her struggles. Several weeks went by without Rozanna mentioning the dark experiences that had been troubling her.

Rozanna's next e-mail removed any doubt as to the status of the warfare that had been tormenting her for her entire life. "Please continue to pray for me. I have not had any peaceful sleep for three months now. Since I have been focusing on a life of total surrender to Jesus, the struggle has been intensifying. Every night horrific dreams fill my mind. Demonic spirits are leaving deep burn marks on my arms and legs with something that feels like hot knives slicing through my skin. People at work have noticed these marks and wonder what has been happening to me. I am exhausted, but I am continuing to trust Jesus for deliverance. I know He will set me free."

We enlisted others to join us in an all-out prayer offensive on Rozanna's behalf. Lesa invited the ladies in her Bible study group to join the prayer offensive. The prayer meeting group following the Bible study joined in a season of special prayer as well. The next week, Wisconsin Camp Meeting began. Lesa and I invited the large group that had come for the early prayer and praise time to join in the prayer offensive. Family members in Arizona were enlisted as well. Pastors and special friends alike joined in special prayer.

As we prayed, God reminded us that the disciples could not cast out the demon in the possessed boy at the bottom of the Mount of Transfiguration. His words sounded clearly in our ears, "This kind does not go out except by prayer and fasting." Some chose to fast and pray as we claimed the power in God's word for Rozanna. The same power in God's living Word that Jesus used to defeat Satan in the wilderness will defeat him today! Many promises such as the one in Isaiah were prayed on Rozanna's behalf.

"Can the prey be taken from the mighty man, or the captives of a tyrant be rescued? Surely, thus says the Lord, even the captives of the mighty man will be taken away, and the prey of the tyrant will be rescued; for I will contend with the one who contends with you" (Isa. 49:24–25).

Rozanna went to bed on Friday night as usual, exhausted and desperately desiring sleep. Reaching over to the alarm clock beside the bed, she set it for 4:30 a.m. for her morning devotions. As she closed her eyes to sleep, she once again entrusted her life to God. The next morning the sun was well into the sky when she opened her eyes. She couldn't believe it. It was 7:30. The dark, oppressive beings had not troubled her even once all night. The presence of evil that had been engulfing her night and day was gone. She felt light hearted and free at last. Her heart overflowed with joyful praise and thanksgiving. Kneeling down before God she wept and wept, tears of thanksgiving running down her cheeks as she lifted up her heart to God in praise. She had been set free from years of oppression. The next night was the same, and the one after, as well. A few nights later she was awakened by one of her unfriendly night visitors. She looked at him and said, "I belong to Jesus," and rolled over and slept peacefully the rest of the night. The power in Jesus' name and blood sacrifice had totally defeated the power of evil.

Rozanna was set free on the Sabbath morning that the early morning camp meeting worshipers joined in prayer. Learning of the wonderful deliverance God had worked for Rozanna, we shared the news with those who had united with us in special prayer. Standing as a group in the main camp meeting tent, we lifted our voices in a joyous expression of worship and praise to One who has forever conquered the devil and his entire host. Lifting our voices in song, and most assuredly supported by an angelic choir, we sang the doxology, praising the God from whom all blessings flow.

Rozanna is rejoicing in the first freedom she has experienced in her forty years of life! Praise the name of Jesus for the amazing victory He gained in the conquest against evil demonstrated at Mount Calvary. The defeat of darkness has been forever assured in the shed blood of Jesus. Some day soon we will be able to thank Him in person for the battle He won for each of us on planet earth. The enemy of souls is forever a defeated foe. Praise the Lord!

If the Creator of the universe filled with planets and stars heard the faint cry of one of His children beaten down by years of dark oppression, don't you think He knows your name as well?

CONCLUSION

—=◉=—

At times life can feel much like it did for the disciples on the stormy Sea of Galilee. Their plans for the future had been dashed to pieces as Jesus dismissed the crowds ready to crown Him king. The multitudes expecting to see them hold governing positions in Jesus' new kingdom had been left behind. Didn't Jesus care how He had made them look? Didn't He care how they felt? How would He ever become king? The way He was going about it, His glorious kingdom would never come.

As the waves lapped against the side of their small fishing boat, their spirits sank lower and lower. Doubt and discouragement led them deeper and deeper down the pathway to despair. Perhaps they had seriously miscalculated the identity and mission of their Master. If He cared at all about their feelings, they most assuredly would not be floating aimlessly across the sea in the middle of the night for no apparent reason. They were drifting further and further from the crowds that had been ready to help them make their dreams a reality. Surely, Jesus had forsaken them!

Without warning the sky and sea assumed the characteristics of their stormy hearts. The howling, shrieking wind whipped the sea into mountains of churning water. Their small fishing boat would surely plunge into the depths at any moment. Surely, Jesus had forgotten their names. Where was He when they needed Him most? The enemy of souls relentlessly pressed his thoughts of discouragement and despair upon these chosen men. From all appearances, they were but one big wave from a watery grave at the bottom of the Sea of Galilee.

In their despair they could not see Jesus, but He had not taken His eye from them for a moment. Standing alone on the shore, He watched the men He had chosen to illuminate the world, like the watchful eye of a mother over her newborn babe. He prayed to His heavenly Father for their troubled hearts. Self-interest had obscured countless demonstrations of His love to them. Jesus had not forgotten them. He had not forsaken them. He was allowing them to see their true condition.

It could be that your life feels like you are about to be swallowed by the next big wave on your own stormy sea. Are discouragement and despair causing you to lose sight of Jesus? In a world filled with painful injustices, it is easy to give in to thoughts and feelings of discouragement. In the end, these feelings will lead to despair and depression. If the father of lies can convince you that you are forgotten and abandoned, you will surely let go of your hold on God. To convince you that you have been forgotten by God is one of the devil's main strategies. In your darkest moments he whispers, "Your name has been misplaced in heaven, and you are on your own!" Feeling alone and forgotten, you will not hold on for long. This highly effective tactic has been used since the very beginning.

I would like the Savior of the world to answer this false assumption once and for all. Listen as He speaks your name personally through His written word: "So that you may know that it is I, the Lord, the God of Israel, who calls you by your name, I have inscribed you on the palms of My hands!" (Isa. 45:3, 16).

When you behold the One hanging alone in the darkness at Calvary, when you behold your name being permanently inscribed into the palms of His hands with the cruel nails fastening Him to the cross, every argument that your name has been forgotten will fall helplessly by the wayside. You are not forgotten, and you never will be! God has promised, "I will never leave you or forsake you," and the inscription of your name in His hands is the eternal evidence that it will always be so (Heb. 13:5).

Here is one more promise from God's Word that I pray you will hear Him speak to you personally: "Remember these things, O *Jacob* (insert your name), and *Israel* (insert your family), for you are My servant. I have formed you; you are My servant, O Israel; *you will not be forgotten by Me.* I have wiped out your transgressions like a thick cloud and your sins like a heavy mist. Return to Me, for I have redeemed you. Shout for joy, O heavens, for the Lord has done it!" (Isa. 44:21-23).

What an amazing God! He has promised that you will remain personally significant throughout eternity; your sins will be removed forever! He personally paid your ransom! Truly, this is reason to shout for joy!

Friend, if you have never surrendered your life to the One who has known your name before you had breath, I invite you to wait not a moment longer. I believe He is calling to you now. An experience you could never have imagined is waiting for you! "I go to prepare a place for you that where I am you may be also"—forever—(John 14:2). Moment by moment, Jesus endured the horrors of Calvary so you would enjoy His personal friendship for eternity. If you do not choose to accept His amazing gift, He will miss you forever. The heart of God longs for your friendship today and throughout the ceaseless tomorrows of eternity.

If the Creator of the vast universe filled with planets and stars would leave His throne in glory to inscribe your name on the palms of His hands, can't you be forever certain that He will never forget your name?

Yes, God *does* know your name and it is my prayer that your understanding of God has been enhanced as you contemplated the life experiences of the individuals in this book.

To order additional copies of

GOD KNOWS
YOUR NAME

Have your credit card ready and call

Toll free: (877) 421-READ (7323)

or order online at: www.winepressbooks.com